Cambridge Elements ≡

Elements in the Philosophy of Religion
edited by
Yujin Nagasawa
University of Birmingham

RELIGIOUS EXPERIENCE

Amber L. Griffioen
University of Notre Dame

CAMBRIDGE
UNIVERSITY PRESS

CAMBRIDGE
UNIVERSITY PRESS

University Printing House, Cambridge CB2 8BS, United Kingdom

One Liberty Plaza, 20th Floor, New York, NY 10006, USA

477 Williamstown Road, Port Melbourne, VIC 3207, Australia

314–321, 3rd Floor, Plot 3, Splendor Forum, Jasola District Centre,
New Delhi – 110025, India

103 Penang Road, #05–06/07, Visioncrest Commercial, Singapore 238467

Cambridge University Press is part of the University of Cambridge.

It furthers the University's mission by disseminating knowledge in the pursuit of
education, learning, and research at the highest international levels of excellence.

www.cambridge.org
Information on this title: www.cambridge.org/9781108742252
DOI: 10.1017/9781108699952

First published 2021

A catalogue record for this publication is available from the British Library.

ISBN 978-1-108-74225-2 Paperback
ISSN 2399-5165 (online)
ISSN 2515-9763 (print)

Religious Experience

Elements in the Philosophy of Religion

DOI: 10.1017/9781108699952
First published online: November 2021

Amber L. Griffioen
University of Notre Dame
Author for correspondence: Amber L. Griffioen, amber.griffs@gmail.com

Abstract: This Element looks at religious experience and the role it has played in philosophy of religion. It critically explores the history of the intertwined discourses on mysticism and religious experience, before turning to a few specific discussions within contemporary philosophy of religion. One debate concerns the question of perennialism versus constructivism and whether there is a "common core" to all religious or mystical experience independent of interpretation or sociohistorical background. Another central discussion concerns the epistemology of purportedly "theophanic" experience and whether a "perceptual model" of religious experience can provide evidence or justification for theistic belief. The Element concludes with a discussion of how philosophy of religion can productively widen its treatment of religious experience in the service of creating a more inclusive and welcoming discipline.

Keywords: religious experience, mysticism, religious epistemology, perennialism, constructivism

ISBNs: 9781108742252 (PB), 9781108699952 (OC)
ISSNs: 2399-5165 (online), 2515-9763 (print)

Contents

Prologue

This Element explores various dimensions of the historical and contemporary philosophical discourse surrounding religious experience. While no text of this length can cover all the material on this topic, my aim here is to present, contextualize, and critique just a few of the central discussions in analytic philosophy of religion as well as to gesture at some new directions a philosophy of religious experience might take that could help correct old biases. Section 1 provides some historical context to the contemporary discourse surrounding religious experience in the Anglo-American and European contexts. Section 2 then looks at one central discussion that came to prominence in the twentieth century, namely whether there is some "common core" to all religious experience and whether such experience can be considered independently of its religious interpretation. In sections 3 and 4, I explore in more detail the epistemology of religious experience, with a particular focus on the analogy drawn by some analytic philosophers between the purported experience of God and sense perception. Finally, Section 5 explores some alternative epistemological approaches to religious experience and concludes with a discussion of the ways the philosophical scholarship on the subject can be fruitfully expanded.

1 Religious and Mystical Experience in Historical Context

The spiritual literature and oral histories of the various world religions are full of reports of the remarkable experiences of noteworthy religious individuals. However, much like the modern concept of religion itself, religious experience did not really become a prominent object of Western academic discourse until the nineteenth century. Indeed, rather like comic book superheroes, discourses surrounding religious experience in philosophy of religion have a (not uncomplicated) "origin story." And just as comic book origin stories help us better understand the motivations, powers, and vulnerabilities of the superheroes we know and love, knowing a bit more about the history of the discourse concerning religious experience can give us important insights into the ways the scholarship is framed today and help us to evaluate both its advantages and its shortcomings.

1.1 A Brief Genealogy of the Discourse

As noted, religious experience itself did not become a topic of philosophical investigation until the modern era. However, *appeals* to religious experience have historically played a significant role in philosophical-theological contexts. (Consider, for example, the centrality of Augustine's conversion experience in the *Confessions*, or Ghazali's being cured of his epistemological paralysis through divine illumination in *Deliverance from Error*.) Further, although many philosophers today tend to associate the high to late Middle Ages in Western Europe with the rise of scholasticism and natural theology, reports of religious experience also became prominent in religious writing during this time as part of a surge in what we today call *religious mysticism*. Many mystical and contemplative texts appeal to instances of divine or saintly encounters to confer legitimacy on the work or its author, and they also often speak of particular kinds of experiential "union" with God as a marker or goal on the individual's spiritual journey (Griffioen and Zahedi 2018). However, the discourse surrounding mysticism has its own complicated history, one which has deeply influenced the philosophical treatment of religious experience down to the present day and which therefore merits a brief discussion here. (For a more detailed analysis, see Jantzen [1995] and Schmidt [2003].)

In Christian antiquity, and persisting through much of the early to high Middle Ages, so-called "mystical theology" had less to do with the experiential aspect of religion and more to do with the *hermeneutical act* of uncovering the "hidden" or "secret" meanings of Scripture and the sacraments (Jantzen 1995). It thus implied having special access to sacred texts and religious secrets, a domain generally reserved for those who enjoyed both literacy and ecclesial power (i.e., *men*). Women were thereby largely excluded from such activity. At the same time, Christianity also had the tools at its disposal to allow religious experience to play a central role in theological reflection. Not only was the Bible full of stories of passive religious encounters such as Moses and the burning bush, the annunciation of Gabriel to Mary, or Saul's conversion on the road to Damascus, medieval Christianity had also developed a long-standing tradition of confessional and meditative theological literature in the first-person voice. Together with the Church's strong veneration of the Virgin Mary as the blessed "handmaid of the Lord" and the dominant Aristotelian view of women as "passive receptacles" largely tied to the body, this paved the way for some later medieval women to lay claim to a certain degree of spiritual authority by appealing to their own passive, ecstatic, and remarkable experiences of the divine to frame and legitimate their theological insights (Van Dyke 2022). Indeed, an upsurge in literacy and the production of devotional literature for the masses during this period allowed both women and laypersons to explicitly enter into theological discourses previously reserved for male scholars by embedding their theological ideas within the context of accounts of their experiential encounters with Christ, Mary, and other holy figures. These forms of contemplative writing allowed the language of personal religious experience to begin to play a greater role in theological and philosophical reflection as a whole.

However, as religious experience gained a more prominent foothold in medieval theological and devotional writing, it also became more heavily policed by the Church – especially when those reporting such experiences were women or members of other socially marginalized groups. Thus, although the term "mystic" came to be more closely associated with religious experience during the late medieval and early modern periods, this terminological shift largely occurred in the context of identifying so-called "false mystics," witches, or heretics (Schmidt 2003). In this way, the earlier hermeneutical sense of mysticism, which was positively connoted yet coded as masculine, gave way to a more gender-inclusive, experiential sense of the term, but one which was negatively associated with unorthodoxy and religious enthusiasm (Jantzen 1994). This shift was accompanied by an increasing *suspicion of somatic and sensory experiences* associated with women, such as religious visions, auditions, stigmata, erotic spiritual encounters, and the like – a suspicion whose vestiges are still visible in the philosophical literature today.

It therefore became all the more important for those worried about being identified as "false mystics" to set out criteria for identifying religious experiences as authentic and to show how their experiences met those criteria, especially given the immensely popular treatises on spiritual discernment by late medieval theologians like Henry of Langenstein and Jean Gerson, who were particularly suspicious of the claims of women and of lay religious sects to authoritative religious experience (Sluhovsky 2007). It was in this context that the sixteenth-century philosopher and Doctor of the Church Teresa of Avila provided strict guidelines for distinguishing divine from hallucinatory, delusional, or demonic experiences in her writings. Cautionary reflections like hers introduced the significance of *evidential considerations* into theological appeals to experience and hence represent a very important chapter in the history of the epistemology of religious experience. And although the epistemological concerns of today's philosophers are far removed from those of Teresa and her contemporaries, we may consider some of the contemporary models of religious experience as having inherited the legacy of these late medieval discourses.

The early modern period in Europe saw a shift in focus to the idea of "rational" or "natural" religion, with the further development of theistic proofs and theodicies by figures like Descartes, Leibniz, Boyle, Clarke, and Paley, as well as discussions of cosmology and the relationship of God to nature by thinkers as diverse as Spinoza, Conway, Malebranche, and the Cambridge Platonists. However, another strand of thought came to prominence with Thomas Reid and Scottish "common sense" philosophy. Reid shifted the discussion from proofs for God's existence to an exploration of the *rationality* of religious belief – and from questions *de facto* to questions *de jure* – a move that would be taken up again by

Reformed epistemologists in the twentieth century and, as we will see, would have a profound impact on the philosophy of religious experience (Nichols 2014).

It also seems to be around this time that mysticism became more solidly linked to claims of direct, ecstatic, ineffable experience of the kind that William James would later point to in his *Varieties of Religious Experience*. Still, at this point in time the use of the term "mysticism" remained largely pejorative. Indeed, the association of mysticism and religious experience with quietism and heretical religious enthusiasm only increased during the Enlightenment, as manifestations of religious fervor came to be seen as antithetical to any acceptable, "rational" form of religion. However, in the eighteenth century, reactionary counter-Enlightenment critics began to speak out against religious rationalism, rebranding those labeled "mystics," not as religious threats, but rather as the guardians of "true religion" (Schmidt 2003: 281). Religion, they maintained, belonged most properly to the experiential realm of *affect*, not intellect, and was most fundamentally a matter of *inner piety*, not the outward actions of individuals, the public activities of the Church, or even the rational defensibility of theological doctrine. These critical responses to the Enlightenment suspicion of mystical experience laid the groundwork for the "invention of mysticism as the fountainhead of all genuine spirituality" that would gain prominence in nineteenth-century German Romanticism and American Transcendentalism (281). In this latter context, the term "mysticism" began to come into its own, bringing religious experience as a subject of scholarly interest along with it.

The shift to viewing feeling and experience as central to the religious enterprise also represented a response to a growing awareness of global religious diversity, one stoked by European missionary and colonialist ventures. On the one hand, this created conceptual space for a more universal(ist) sense of religion that promoted a degree of religious tolerance and would set the stage for modern scholarly approaches to religion. On the other hand, it often ended up binding disparate traditions together under a particular *essentialist* conceptual umbrella – one driven largely by European theological and imperialist norms (Asad 1993). Still, this "experiential turn" in the scholarship of religion gave rise to the thought of those figures most commonly referenced today in the philosophical literature on religious experience.

1.2 The Experiential Turn: Schleiermacher, Otto, and James

Three names occur again and again in the contemporary literature, namely Friedrich Schleiermacher (1768–1834), Rudolf Otto (1869–1937), and William James (1842–1910). Schleiermacher and Otto, both Protestant German theologians, tend to be named in the same breath – especially in debates over perennialism, which we shall take up below – whereas James, the philo-sophical pragmatist and pioneer of religious psychology, remains a major touchstone for both empirical and philosophical approaches to religious experi-ence. As we shall see, despite their different approaches to religious experience, the literature's combined reliance on these three figures has led to the philo-sophical discourse on religious experience being largely framed in a particular way.

1.2.1 Friedrich Schleiermacher (1768–1834): Religion as Feeling

Schleiermacher's thoughts on religious experience and feeling evolved over his lifetime, but the passages most commonly cited refer, first, to his claim in the *Speeches on Religion* (1st ed. 1799) that "religion is the sensibility and taste for the infinite" (1996: 23) and, second, to his much later discussion in §4 of *The Christian Faith* (1821/1822), in which he claims that "the common element in all howsoever diverse expressions of [religious] piety, by which these are conjointly distinguished from all other feelings [. . .] is this: the consciousness of being absolutely depend-ent, or, which is the same thing, of being in relation with God" (2016: 12).

Consonant with the emerging resistance to the attempts of modernity to reduce religion to either doctrine or morality, Schleiermacher thus claimed that religious piety was a deliverance of neither intellect nor will but rather something direct and immediate, not framed by conceptual thought, which can only be understood by acquaintance (Proudfoot 1985: 10–11). This grounding of religion in a particular form of feeling (*Gefühl*) is decidedly experiential. The emphasis here is not on what a particular subject thinks or does, but rather something they *feel*, something that is *given* to them in experience, whether or not they can articulate it. In one sense, this emphatic centering of affect should come as no surprise, given the blossoming of German Romanticism taking place at this time in Schleiermacher's own intellectual circle. Nevertheless, this idea turned the Lutheran theology of his day "on its head," insofar as he maintained that religious feeling represented the very *basis* for religious belief and theological doctrine, as opposed to the other way around – so much so that Jacqueline Mariña goes so far as to call Schleiermacher's insistence that feeling lies at the core of all religion a "Copernican revolution in theology" (2008: 461).

1.2.2 Rudolf Otto: Religion, Experience, and the Numinous

Although his most influential work, *Das Heilige* (1917), translated as *The Idea of the Holy* (1923), was written nearly a century after Schleiermacher's *Glaubenslehre*, Rudolf Otto explicitly acknowledged his indebtedness to

Schleiermacher's approach, even while taking him to task for what he claimed to be an inadequate account of the genuinely religious "moment" in human experience. Like Schleiermacher, Otto took the religious impulse to properly belong to the realm of feeling, and he placed the category of value expressed in that feeling outside the realm of the theoretical and moral. This element of "more profound" religion, when stripped of all its "rational[ized]" aspects, Otto famously called the *Numinous*. It represents, he thought, a "completely sui generis" category that is not, strictly speaking, definable or teachable, but rather only capable of being "evoked" or "awakened" in consciousness (Otto 2004: 7ff.). "Numinous," then, is a label for both the *object* and the *quality* of the religious *Ur-moment*.

The core numinous experience, which stands at the heart of the so-called "nonrational" aspects of lived religion, Otto claims, takes as its object something purportedly "not explicable in concepts [and] only specifiable through the special reaction in feeling that it elicits" (2004: 13). More specifically, the subject experiences the Numinous as *mysterium tremendum et fascinans*. As *mysterium tremendum*, the Numinous is met with feelings of awe and dread at that which is apprehended as "the Wholly Other" (*das Ganz Andere*), whose utter transcendence pushes the subject away or evokes feelings of radical distance. At the same time, as *fascinans*, the Numinous fascinates, attracts, and draws the subject to it. Otto takes this ineffable, paradoxical experience of awful dread and fascination – like the "irrational" object that elicits it – to be sui generis and irreducible to other forms of feeling, even if related "analogously" to other, more easily recognizable emotions. (He seems to think that the uniqueness of the numinous object demands this.) And since this experience stands genealogically at the core of all religion, it is also that which serves to transform empirical, historical religion into a more or less universal, sui generis phenomenon.

1.2.3 William James: An Empirical Approach

When it was published in 1902, William James' *The Varieties of Religious Experience* was one of the lengthiest and most detailed scholarly treatments of religious experience produced up to that time. In line (though not exactly in step) with Schleiermacher and Otto, James was concerned with countering overly rationalistic, intellectualist, and institutionalist narratives about religion, hence his focus on what he calls "personal religion" and its association with experience, feeling, and emotion. He was nevertheless careful to note the relative arbitrariness of his own definition of religion as "*the feelings, acts, and experiences of individual[s] in their solitude, so far as they apprehend themselves to stand in relation to whatever they may consider the divine"* (James 2002: 29–30, emphasis original).

However, despite making feeling and experience central to religion, James did *not* subscribe to the view that there is a common phenomenological core to all religious experiences. He noted that there "seems to be no one elementary religious emotion, but only a common storehouse of emotions upon which religious objects may draw." Moreover, *pace* Otto, "there might conceivably also prove to be no one specific and essential kind of religious object" that would elicit some sui generis religious experience (James 2002: 27). In this spirit, James presents the reader with a multitude of cases taken from various world religions and historical epochs, and although he did tend to focus on their commonalities over their differences, he was careful to maintain a sense of pluralism throughout. Still, the examples James gives his readers are nonetheless filtered through an admittedly Western, Protestant lens and are often taken largely out of their social and historical contexts. He was also most concerned with the experiences of those he calls religious "geniuses," as opposed to "ordinary" believers who only live "second-hand" religious lives (11).

James' normative individualism in the *Varieties* had no small effect on a wide range of later philosophical and psychological texts regarding religious experience up to the present day (Jantzen 1995; Bush 2014), and this has further served to universalize and genericize certain kinds of religious experience while marginalizing others. Indeed, it is somewhat ironic that James' attempt to particularize and pluralize religious experience has been used again and again to reinforce a particular kind of subjective, individual experience as paradigm, while eschewing others as "suspect," "superstitious," or simply not worth investigating.

More than any other discussion in the *Varieties*, it is the chapter on mysticism that has garnered the most attention from scholars of religion. Although, as with his definition of religion above, he admits his criteria are relatively arbitrary, James proposed four "marks" of mystical experience – namely, *ineffability, noetic quality, transiency*, and *passivity* (2002: 295). That is, such experiences seem to those who have them as incapable of straightforward expression, as states of knowledge or as knowledge-conferring, as episodic and temporally unsustainable, and as something with regard to which one is wholly passive. While James intended this rubric to pick out only one cluster of experiences "for the purposes of the present lectures," these characteristics have been taken up by philosophers, theologians, and religious scholars in the generations that followed, and it has often been implied, especially in philosophy of religion, that experiences of this kind are pretty much the only kinds of religious experiences worth discussing.

1.2.4 Schleiermacher, Otto, and James in Conversation

Certainly there is much that unites these three thinkers. For example, their analyses all largely eschew approaches that center the institutional or the doctrinal, as well as those that attempt to reduce religion to either metaphysics or morals. Instead, they focus on the passivity with respect to some higher reality as given to the subject in experience, and they orient their discussions of religion around religious feeling. They all also focus, in one way or another, on individual religious "virtuosi" or "geniuses," where what is seen to lie at the heart of religion comes most prominently to expression in intense moments of profound episodic experience (Joas 2011: 157).

However, there are also important differences between Schleiermacher, Otto, and James that tend to be ignored or elided in the religious experience literature. For example, Schleiermacher and Otto are also often clustered together as proponents of a "sui generis" account of religious feeling. Yet this ignores the fundamentally *transcendental* character of Schleiermacher's account of the feeling of absolute dependence and may actually have more to do with Otto's self-styling as Schleiermacher's intellectual heir than with an actual continuity in thought (Mariña 2008; Dole 2016). Moreover, Otto was a vehement non-naturalist, whereas Schleiermacher was perhaps much more sympathetic to a form of tempered naturalism (Dole 2004, 2016), placing the latter closer in this respect to James, who insisted that our ability to provide a naturalistic explanation for religious experiences precluded neither their psychological import nor their veridicality.

In contrast to both Schleiermacher and Otto, James emerges from a distinctly American experiential tradition, one that included the American Transcendentalists as well as figures like Cotton Mather and Jonathan Edwards (Joas 2011). He also pursues an explicitly empirical agenda and is an avowed pluralist about religious experience. Still, as Ann Taves has rightly pointed out, although James did not advocate for a sui generis account of religion or religious experience, by privileging the extreme experience of the religious "genius" over that of the everyday believer, he nevertheless "introduced a bias toward sudden, individual experience that [. . .] shaped the contemporary Western idea of religious experience" (Taves 2009: 6). Especially when paired with Otto's detailed phenomenological analysis of the "sudden, individual experience" of *mysterium tremendum et fascinans*, James' approach would have an impact on philosophers and theologians for generations to come.

Indeed, the discussion over whether the essence of Jamesian-style religious experiences is cross-cultural and irreducible would give rise to one of the central conceptual debates that would dominate much of the discussion on religious experience in the century to come, namely the discourse on the relationship between *experience* and *interpretation* and its bearing on the question of whether we can really speak of there being a "common core" to the wide variety of religious experiences of the kind explored by James and others. We will turn our attention more closely to these questions in Section 2, keeping in mind the tendencies of the discourse to privilege certain sorts of experience over others.

2 Experience, Interpretation, and the Question of Perennialism

In the twentieth century, psychology, neuroscience, and the social sciences began to emerge more fully as distinct disciplines, bringing new methods and approaches to the growing Western fascination with world religions (itself due in no small part to the spread of colonialism). In the context of this increasingly "global" outlook, new debates also began to emerge regarding the nature of religion. Given the various ways the essence or significance of religion had come to be associated with religious feeling, this raised new questions regarding the nature of religious experience.

2.1 Experience, Essentialism, and Perennialism

One of the central discussions in this arena of discourse revolved around (a) whether or not there is some common experiential "core" fundamental to all religion, and (b) whether religious experiences across time, culture, and place have some common (usually phenomenal) element that unites them. Importantly, these two questions are not the same. The first asks whether the core of religion itself can be located in some particular type of experience and concerns what we might call the question of *experiential essentialism* about religion. The second asks whether there is some universal feature of religious experience common to all traditions, regardless of its centrality to any particular tradition. This we can call the question of *experiential perennialism*. In many cases, those who answer the latter question in the affirmative will also answer the former affirmatively, and vice versa. But these views can and do come apart. Unfortunately, some scholars in these debates have failed to distinguish between these questions, which has sometimes led to confusion. For the sake of space, I will focus predominantly on views addressing the second question, though in some cases the affirmative perennialist answer to this question is driven by a motivation to establish essentialism concerning religion in general (McCutcheon 1997).

On the perennialist side of the debate, various answers have been proposed. We have already seen Rudolf Otto's proposal that religious experience involves the sui generis feeling of *mysterium tremendum et fascinans*. For Otto, what makes this experience specifically *religious* has to do with its having a singular, properly religious *object* (i.e., the Numinous). Any experience of this religious object will, by virtue of the object's singular nature, have a particular phenomenology that will distinguish it from all nonreligious experience. So unlike other emotion-types, whose appropriateness is measured according to how well the affective response "fits" the nature of the target, on Otto's view there is only *one* target that can be the object of the religious feeling and one feeling that can represent the response to that target. Any other target would result, not in an inappropriate religious feeling, but in a *nonreligious* feeling. On this view, then, it would seem that there could be no such thing as an "inappropriate" token of religious emotion, in which the experiential response fails to fit the target.

Many perennialists have found inspiration in Otto – often in the spirit of a kind of religious inclusivity or theological universalism. If it could be shown, for example, that there is some common religious experience that lies at the core of all world religions (i.e., that both experiential perennialism and experiential essentialism about religion are true), then this might be one way of showing that they are ultimately more in agreement than in substantial conflict. Moreover, if one proceeds on the assumption that these common religious experiences also share a common *object*, as Otto proposes, this might open the door for the idea that subjects outside one's own religious tradition could also have experiential knowledge of a kind relevant for salvation, or that all religions have an at least partial glimpse of some greater redemptive or transformative "Truth."

Another influential proponent of experiential perennialism is Mircea Eliade (1907–1986), whose work has been extremely important for the phenomenology of religion. Like Otto, he was also a proponent of experiential essentialism about religion. (The subtitle of Eliade's most famous work, *The Sacred and the Profane* [1959], is *The Nature of Religion*.) Although Eliade thought that various types of experiences could represent instances of "hierophany," or the "showing" of something sacred to the human individual (1987: 10–11), the view remains perennialist insofar as the religious "mode" of experiencing across geography and history involves a qualitatively different *way* of being oriented toward and experiencing reality, namely *as manifesting the sacred* in some way or other. Eliade's work draws on a plethora of examples from various cultures and historical periods, but ultimately he was concerned with showing that "in the course of history, religious man has given differing valorizations to the *same fundamental experience*" (62, my emphasis). And although he admits that historical and cultural context does matter, he nevertheless emphasizes that the experiential structure of hierophanies "remains the same in spite of this and it is precisely this permanence of structure that makes it possible to know them" (Eliade 1958: 462).

In contrast to Otto, however, what makes an experience religious for Eliade is the subjective manner in which some aspect of reality is experienced, not necessarily the unique nature of the object of the experience. We may therefore be better able to understand Eliade's theory as a kind of "adverbial" account of religious experience ("experiencing sacredly"), such that we can draw a distinction between Otto's and Eliade's perennialism. While both maintain that there is some universal, irreducible, common core to both religious experience and religion, for Otto the phenomenology of the experience is a byproduct of the singular religious object, whereas Eliade allows that the experience can frame and structure, perhaps even in some sense constitute, the reality it perceives. Hence, Eliade claims, the person who experiences the sacred as manifesting itself in a hierophany establishes in this experience a fixed point of orientation, and this "discovery or projection of a fixed point – the center – is equivalent to the creation of the world" (1987: 21–22).

Other perennialist strategies take less of an armchair phenomenological approach, adopting a page from James' playbook and appealing to empirical reports of experiences they take to be of a certain kind. Still, these approaches differ remarkably from one another – and, in some cases, from James' approach itself. For example, one of the early pioneers of the study of mysticism, Evelyn Underhill (1875–1941), rejected James' famous four features of mystical experience (ineffability, noetic quality, transiency, and passivity), claiming that "true mysticism is active and practical, not passive and theoretical" (1912: 96). Still, she insisted that "Mysticism entails a definite Psychological Experience" involving both "the vision or consciousness of Absolute Perfection" and an "inward transmutation to which that Vision compels the mystic" (107–108). This "impassioned love of the Absolute," she claimed, "transcends the dogmatic language in which it is clothed and becomes applicable to mystics of every race and creed" (103).

W.T. Stace (1886–1967), who also focused largely on reports of mystical experience, distinguished between two kinds that he took to be universal, namely "extrovertive" mystical experience (which "looks outward," sometimes through the senses) and "introvertive" mystical experience (which "looks inward into the mind"). However, he viewed extrovertive sensory experience as no more than a "stepping stone to the higher introvertive state" and ultimately "of less importance" (Stace 1960: 49). Indeed, in keeping with the historical suspicion of bodily experience, Stace explicitly excludes visions, voices, raptures, trances, "hyperemotionalism," and other essentially somatic experiences, stipulating that "the most typical as well as the most important type of mystical experience is *nonsensuous*" and going so far as to state that "excessive emotionalism [. . .] is, according to this writer's taste, an unpalatable characteristic, tending to show lack of balance and of good judgment and critical ability" (49). Introvertive experiences, on the other hand, of which Stace thinks "there is no doubt that in essence they are the same all over the world in all cultures, religions, places, and ages," achieve a "complete vacuum of particular mental contents, [...] a state of *pure* consciousness [which] has no content except itself" (85–86). More recently, psychologist Ralph Hood (2001) has drawn on Stace's categorizations to develop a "mysticism scale" for use in empirical studies of mystical experience and has maintained that there is good empirical evidence to conclude on the basis of these categories that there is some common phenomenological core to mystical experience. Of course, his use of Stace's categories as his point of departure might make one worry that Hood has stacked the deck in favor of the perennialist approach.

Other, somewhat more pluralist-minded thinkers divide up perennial mystical or religious experience into more categories than Stace's dualist extrovertive-introvertive schema. For example, the late Keith Yandell (1938–2020), although doubting that all religious experiences everywhere have some single object or intrinsic structure, developed a "modest typology" of what he considered epistemologically relevant religious experience, dividing it into *monotheistic, nirvanic, kevalic, moksha,* and *nature* experiences in *The Epistemology of Religious Experience* (1993). Still others have admitted that there may be various species of religious experience, while claiming that only one of them is universal across religions. For example, another thinker who discounts sensory mystical experience, Robert K. C. Forman, nevertheless admits that there are various sorts of "important" mystical phenomena. Still, his focus is on "one quite interesting and relatively common form," namely what he calls a *pure consciousness event,* or PCE (Forman 1999: 6–7). This "experience" (or, perhaps more accurately, "anti-experience") is described as a subject's being "awake, conscious, but without an object or content for consciousness – no thoughts, emotions, sensations, or awareness of any external phenomena" (Forman 1986: 49).

There are thus many varieties of experiential religious perennialism. What the above theorists have in common, however, is that by and large they agree that there is at least one type or manifestation of religious experience that (i) displays some common, usually phenomenal, feature among individuals from different times, places, and cultures, and (ii) is independent of, prior to, and/or more fundamental than the interpretation of those experiences. That is, they tend to agree with Ninian Smart (1927–2001) that, phenomenologically, these experiences are "everywhere the same," even if "different flavours" accrue to the them because of the experiencing subjects' differing cultural and hermeneutical backgrounds (1965: 87).

2.2 Constructivism and the Question of Interpretation

A countervailing approach arose largely in response to the sharp division that perennialist approaches tended to draw between the "core" experience and its interpretation, as well as to the not unrelated claim that religious experience is, most fundamentally, *acultural, ahistorical,* and *preconceptual.* Influential proponents of this critical approach, such as Steven Katz and Wayne Proudfoot, have argued that experience cannot be viewed as independent from the concepts that give it shape. Insofar as our concepts largely or wholly depend on the social contexts in which we find ourselves, religious experience will always be fundamentally socioculturally and historically informed. In keeping with the literature, let us call this approach *experiential constructivism,* though the term "constructivism" seems to have been foisted on its proponents by its critics. (Nowhere in Proudfoot's [1985] *Religious Experience* does he refer to his view this way, and Katz [1992] explicitly eschews the label, preferring instead to describe himself as a "contextualist.") Experiential constructivism stands as the scholarly foil to experiential perennialism and is thus also to be distinguished from *experiential anti-essentialism* about religion. However, much of the constructivist literature with respect to religious experience is motivated by a resistance to both experiential perennialism and uncritical religious essentialism.

For example, Katz worries that although much early perennialism was motivated by an "ecumenical desire," it also tended to be accompanied by a "dogmatic consideration" – one still bound up with early missionary efforts – which claims that "all religions, even if appearing different, really teach *x,*" where the content of *x* is provided by "the particular dogmatic beliefs the given interpreter happens to hold" (1978: 24). In so doing, the perennialist scholar ensures conformance with their favored religious perspective by dismissing purported divergences in experience as a matter of either superficial difference or straightforward misinterpretation. Even more nuanced perennialists, Katz thinks, still end up being "too reductive and inflexible," insofar as they force "multifarious and extremely variegated forms of mystical experience into improper interpretative categories which lose sight of the fundamentally important differences between the data studied" (25). He then takes Stace and company to task for cherry-picking similar-sounding examples from multiple traditions while taking them out of their social and historical contexts and forcing them into a preconceived perennialist mold, thereby threatening to make these experiences almost unrecognizable in the subject's own milieu. Katz's "plea for the recognition of differences" (25), however, is not merely reactionary. He also claims that, *pace* PCE-perennialists like Forman, "*there are no pure (i.e. unmediated) experiences*" and that mystical experience is always "shaped by concepts which the mystic brings to [...] his experience" (26). For Katz, the relationship between religious experience and religious belief is never unidirectional: "beliefs shape experience, just as experience shapes belief" (30). He thus proposes that a more pluralistic account of mystical experience is necessary.

Proudfoot, too, is worried that the perennialist ends up distorting religious experiences by favoring sameness over difference and universality over diversity: "An experience must be specified under a description that can be ascribed to the subject," he writes, and often "we discover that our anachronistic readings have prevented our understanding the terms in which people identified their experience" (1985: 185). Like Katz, Proudfoot maintains that the prior concepts subjects bring with them, as well as the cultural backgrounds that inform those concepts, play a noneliminable role in the shaping of all experience, including religious experience. However, he still wants to be able to provide some sort of account concerning how we are to classify an experience as specifically *religious*. With James, Proudfoot agrees that religious experience has some sort of "noetic quality or epistemic element," which he identifies with an assumption or belief on the part of the subject that a wholly naturalistic account of their experience is insufficient to explain it. And while he admits that there are "mystical regimens and other disciplines for prayer and meditation that powerfully affect both mind and body," he thinks such practices are taken to be mere "catalysts," not sufficient explanations, for the experience: "If it was thought that an experience could be exhaustively explained by these manipulations," he claims, "then it could not be apprehended by the subject as religious" (187–188).

However, even if Proudfoot thinks we need to take subjects' accounts of their experiences at their word to understand what makes them religious, he is nevertheless open to forms of explanatory reduction from the outside, where "the terms of the explanation need not be familiar or acceptable to the subject" and in which "the explanandum is set in a new context, whether that be one of covering laws and initial conditions, narrative structure, or some other explanatory model" (1985: 197). This strategy allows scholars of religion to take seriously the descriptions of religious experiences by the subjects who have undergone them while at the same time not begging the question against naturalistic accounts of religious experience. It also lends itself well to feminist and critical approaches, insofar as it can account for the ways in which religious experience may be shaped by, for example, sex-role differentiation in religious practice or oppressive conceptions of value, without thereby denying the religious significance of the experience to the subject themself (Raphael 1994).

Other scholars criticize the perennialist position for what is construed as a problematic tendency to erase difference in favor of an approach to religion that upholds particular hegemonial, colonial, or patriarchal norms. Russell McCutcheon, for example, claims that although it tends to be experiential perennialists who are "yelling loudest" about taking religion seriously, it is exactly these theorists who have demonstrated the least seriousness with respect to their relatively uncritical essentialist use of the term "religion" which, McCutcheon argues, has been largely shaped by Western ideals and values (2012: 23). For many perennialist essentialists, he argues, religious experience has been taken to be the a priori *explanans* for religion, not itself a publicly accessible *explanandum* in need of deconstruction or analysis.

Indeed, on such a view it is not just terms like "religion" and "religious" that are socially constructed. As Joan Wallach Scott points out, scholars of religion also need to reflect carefully on the ways the term "experience" itself has been constructed in the history of Western scholarship. Experience, she claims, should not be "the origin of our explanation, but that which we want to explain" (Scott 1991: 797). In this spirit, scholars like Robert Sharf have argued that the common perennialist idea of experience as something private, subjective, and inaccessible to others itself betrays a bias toward a certain Western, Cartesian view of selfhood and unassailable first-person knowledge (1998: 111). The idea that religious studies takes as its object "the inner experience of religious practitioners," he thinks, is both mistaken and indicative of a particular ideology. For Sharf, there is little reason for religious scholars to go looking "behind" the texts, narratives, performances, etc. of religious adherents to retrieve some purportedly sui generis experiential "core" of religion – one which is, by fiat, claimed to be private and ultimately empirically inaccessible to anyone besides the experiencing subject themself. Yet, as Scott points out, even if such reflections might tempt one to give up on the term "experience" altogether, it is such an ineliminable part of our everyday vocabulary that we should perhaps instead "work with it, to analyze its operations and to redefine its meaning" (1991: 797). Importantly, however, she thinks we must always remain aware that "experience is at once always already an interpretation and something that needs to be interpreted. What counts as experience is neither self-evident nor straightforward; it is always contested, and always therefore political" (797).

2.3 Perennialism and Constructivism in Comparison

Much of the divide between perennialists and constructivists hinges on their approach to the role of *concepts* in religious experience. For the perennialist, experience and conceptual mediation can and do come apart. For the constructivist, experience is always saturated with or framed by concepts from a subject's historical and sociocultural context, such that experience and interpretation are never neatly separable. Moreover, the emphasis for the perennialist will tend to be on the qualitative character of the subject's purportedly private experience, whereas the constructivist's focus will be on the collective and publicly accessible conditions that inform and shape the subject's experience.

Perennialist theories have one potential advantage over constructivist approaches in being able to better explain what it is that makes a religious experience *religious*, at least insofar as the kind of experience they point to is taken to be qualitatively unique. The constructivist will usually need some independent account of religion or religiosity to be able to append the term "religious" to an experience, a requirement that the perennialist can better sidestep by appealing to religious experience as an *explanans* as opposed to *explanandum*. Of course, the constructivist is likely to respond that the perennialist is begging the question in favor of certain kinds of experience, a charge that – at least from an empirical standpoint – it would seem the perennialist must address. Perennialist theories also allow for the possibility that one could be ignorant of having had a religious experience (assuming such experiences are not self-verifying), since experience and interpretation can come apart. This might allow for the possibility that subjects, including atheists or agnostics, could have religious experiences and simply not realize it. On the constructivist account, one might be unaware of the way religious concepts shape one's experience or ignorant of the historical religious origins of the concepts that frame one's thinking, but this would be a different kind of "latent religiosity" than that proposed by the perennialist. Finally, if one is searching for a way to resolve religious disagreement or show that religious differences are merely superficial (e.g., in the pursuit of interreligious understanding or the resolution of religious conflict), perennialism provides a way for scholars to unite religious traditions under a single experiential umbrella. However, in emphasizing universal sameness over plurality, many perennialist views also threaten to grossly misinterpret or distort the very religions they wish to bring together and to potentially elide important differences between religious traditions.

Constructivist views, on the other hand, are better able to account for religious plurality, and to take seriously religious difference and the importance of social-historical-cultural situatedness. They further demonstrate the significance of a subject's or community's historical, geographical, and cultural standpoint in the shaping of experience, which can be important when attempting to conduct sincere interreligious dialogue. Contemporary constructivists also are careful to recognize that religious scholars' use of terms like "religion" and "experience" themselves have a history and that this history can bias those studying religion and religious experience in certain ways. At the same time, if one's constructivism leads to a kind of strong religious relativism positing a radical incommensurability between the forms of life we label "religious," this may threaten the very possibility of meaningful religious theorizing or interfaith dialogue. At the very least, it would require the location or development of a negotiated "meta-language" between traditions or the use of boundary-crossing mediators or religious "translators" to get off the ground.

2.4 A Way Through?

The debate between perennialists and constructivists, while still current, has made little progress in recent years. Philosophers of religion interested in epistemological issues have often tried to sidestep the debate as best they can, since fully embracing either side could be problematic for their epistemological projects. There have, however, been some attempts to productively move past (or "through") the perennialist-constructivist debate. These views may help us better take seriously the insights of both approaches moving forward, even if many of the discussions which follow do not require a final settling of the question.

2.4.1 The Two-Realms View: Critical Realism and Religious Experience

One influential view that walks the "tightrope" between perennialism and constructivism (and has been alternately labeled as both) can be found in *critical realist* approaches like that of John Hick (1922–2012). To begin, Hick notes that the various world religions generally agree that one important criterion for identifying an authentic religious experience has to do with its production of moral and spiritual "fruits." Moreover, he thinks that they are also more or less "on a par in respect of these fruits" (Hick 2006: 163). Of course, the perennialist is looking for some common element in all religious experience itself, not merely for a general trend in its effects. Yet Hick's central thesis comes much closer to the perennialist view than one might at first expect. In a quasi-Kantian move, he argues for a distinction between the "Real" or "Transcendent in itself" and its phenomenal appearance as an object of human experience and interpretation. Thus, it is not merely the transformative effects of religious experiences that unite them across time and culture but also the fact that each of these experiences itself represents a *response* to some universally present "Transcendent Reality" (Hick 1989: 240) – a move that contains vestiges of Otto's "Numinous." Still, Hick is careful to claim that the varieties of phenomenal religious experience that represent a response to this "hidden

Transcendent" are largely determined by cultural background and historical context, as on the constructivist view. Indeed, for Hick, "meaning is always couched at least partly in terms that exceed the immediately given" (136), and all experiencing is, even if only on a preconscious level, a matter of interpretation or "experiencing-as" (141). In this way, Hick's view preserves certain central perennialist and constructivist intuitions, so long as the former is willing to move away from a purely phenomenological account of religious experience and the latter is willing to adopt Hick's critical realist metaphysics.

2.4.2 The Building-Block Approach: Experiences Deemed Religious

In *Religious Experience Reconsidered* (2009), Ann Taves raises a concern about strong constructivist views, namely that they fail to take seriously the reports of subjects who insist that their experiences go beyond what their cultural context or previous theological education had primed them for. The possibility that culture cannot always adequately account for the shape of these subjects' experiences – and that they may indeed "challenge our expectations and give rise to novelties" – suggests that a strong constructivist view may not be sufficient to explain the phenomena (97–98). At the same time, Taves also challenges the claims of those who use their perennialism to ground a form of experiential essentialism that "sets the study of religion apart and protects it with taboos against comparing it with nonreligious things" (14). A more promising approach, she thinks, is one that would "situate the processes whereby people characterize things as religious, mystical, magical, and so forth within larger processes of meaning making and valuation," such that religious experience would not be something that "sets the study of religion apart from all other forms of knowledge but rather locates it in relation to them" (64).

Taves' own historically and empirically informed "attributivist" account argues for an embodied, interactive approach to religious experience – one which shifts the discourse from the rather vague term "religious experience" to the more concrete category of "experiences deemed religious" (2009: 93). Her approach encourages scholars of religion to focus both on the *plurality* of experiences in religion and the role played by individuals in "deeming" them religious by attempting to make space for both "top-down or conceptually driven" cognitive processing and "bottom-up or data-driven" (typically unconscious) processing in the psychological analyses of such experiences (62). This allows that religious experiences may sometimes be more heavily interpretive in nature and sometimes seem to reveal new information to the subject. This is not so much a "middle ground" between constructivism and perennialism but rather, as Taves herself puts it, a *reframing* of the debate "in terms of the *interaction* and *relative importance* of top-down (culture sensitive) and bottom-up (culture insensitive) processing in relation to particular experiences" (93).

Taves argues for "disaggregating" religious experience and studying how it is that anything, including experience, ends up being deemed religious, as well as how those simple things and events deemed religious can serve as "building blocks" in the evolution of the more complex, composite social formations we tend to call "religions" or "spiritualities" (2009: 9). This, of course, requires saying something about what it means for something to be "deemed" religious, who does the deeming, and which experiences are to be studied. With respect to the term "religious," given both its ambiguity and its association with Western-centric notions of "religion," Taves prefers to speak instead of attributions of *specialness*, an idea inspired by the Durkheimian notion of "sacredness" or "being set apart" that can take the form of, for example, *ideal* or *anomalous* things and events (45). Ascriptions ("deemings") of specialness, for their part, may be made by both individuals and groups, and they may be "simple" (i.e., applied to particular instances and events) or "composite" (i.e., having to do with entire *paths* deemed special, "whereby the special thing [. . .] may be re-created, re-encountered, and thus re-experienced in the present" [54]). Experiences, then, represent only one of many possible objects that "deeming special" or "setting apart" can take, and Taves chooses to focus specifically on those which are discrete, episodic, remarkable, take an intentional object, and for which "consciousness" can be used as a rough synonym (57). Importantly, however, she notes that experience should not (and perhaps cannot) be studied without involving intersubjective interaction and the subject making their experience *public* in some way. The study of experiences deemed religious, too, needs to be "interactive" and "conversationally based" (87).

Of course, Taves nowhere insists that this is the *only* or even the *best* way to approach either religion or experience, even from within her own attributional approach. This leaves the door open for other scholars to take what is useful from her approach and apply it in other contexts, and she challenges future scholars to "refine" the marks and types of specialness she sets out, adding others "as needed to reflect what they find in various contexts" (Taves 2009: 163). Her approach thus represents an important move in scholarly discussions of religious experience.

2.4.3 The Social-Practical Model: A Holistic Approach

In *Visions of Religion: Experience, Meaning, and Power* (2014), Stephen Bush develops a social-practical approach to religion, as opposed to a purely experiential one, according to which religion, like other social practices, is understood as involving "a shared pattern of behavior [. . .] conducted according to norms" (3). *Pace* many perennialists, Bush thinks that phenomenology will be insufficient to get at what religious experience is, and that "one's background beliefs and attitudes count too" (146). At the same time, Bush is concerned that Taves' "building-block" approach to religion is too piecemeal, insofar as it involves thinking of any particular religious experience (or other religious element) as something "distinct and self-contained [. . .] that retains its nature regardless of how it is arranged or rearranged in larger configurations" (157). His own view, he claims, takes both meaning and significance to be *holistically* determined, such that – even in the case of a simple ascription of "specialness" – an experience's significance is determined by the role it plays in religious practice, as well as in any other social practices that may intersect with it in a particular context. Moreover, on Bush's account, there is an essentially *public* and *discursive* side to the very having of a religious experience. Having a religious experience, he thinks, involves acquiring dispositions "to speak, infer, and act in certain ways," including to *report* that experience using "terms that one has acquired through socialization and language learning," as well as expecting to be "held responsible by one's conversation partners" (145). Thus, not only does religious experience necessarily deploy concepts, this deployment is understood less as a private mental event and more as the exercise of intersubjective dispositions which are socially and culturally primed.

Bush's social-practical model obviously favors the constructivist position over the perennialist one. Yet it retains several key perennialist intuitions. For example, although he denies experiential essentialism *about* religion, he thinks experience plays an extremely important, noneliminable role *in* religion. Moreover, like Hick, he clears the way for a kind of *nonphenomenological perennialism* that could invoke common causal processes or some other "universal" feature in the *mechanics* of religious experiences across cultures. Of course, Bush's central aim is not to resolve the perennialist-constructivist debate but rather to show the ways in which experience, meaning, and power are *all* central to the study of religion and the various ways in which they and the discourses surrounding them are inextricably intertwined, a fact unfortunately ignored by much of the contemporary philosophical literature on religious experience. Indeed, even if one doesn't want to go all-in with Bush's "social-practice" model, one can nevertheless accept the insight that philosophy of religion scholars must take into account the roles that both *hermeneutics* and *social power relations* play in the construction, interpretation, and designation of religious experience.

Bush's approach also takes seriously what John Cottingham has called *the primacy of praxis* in religion. "It is in the very nature of religious understanding," Cottingham writes, "that it characteristically stems from practical involvement rather than from intellectual analysis" (2005: 6). We will return to the importance of religious practice in Section 5 below. However, even if (to channel Abraham Heschel) praise precedes proof for most actual religious adherents, the bulk of philosophers working on religious experience over the past fifty years have tended to focus on the *noetic* aspects of religious experience and what they mean for the rationality of theistic belief. For this reason, it will be important to examine more closely a couple of the ways religious experience has been put to use in analytic religious epistemology and the debates to which this treatment has given rise.

3 Religious Experience as Perception of God: Theistic Approaches

As analytic philosophy of religion shifted its focus from questions concerning religious language in the mid-twentieth century to more extended metaphysical discussions and defenses of perfect-being theology from the 1970s onward, philosophers in this tradition began to turn their attention from questions surrounding perennialism to the potential *epistemic value* of religious experience. As in many of the debates concerning perennialism, however, religious epistemologists have predominantly focused their discussions on numinous, theistic experiences that roughly correspond to the Jamesian framework for mystical experience discussed above. That is, they have tended to center episodic, passive, remarkable experiences taken specifically to be *of God*. Following Evan Fales (1996a), we may think of such experiences as representing purported "theophanies" or "showings" of God. I will thus refer to them in what follows as *theophanic experiences*.

While philosophers have often either disagreed about or simply ignored James' most prominent criterion for mystical experience, namely ineffability, for better or worse they seem to overwhelmingly agree (or at least strongly insinuate) that the most philosophically interesting feature of such experiences is their purported *noetic quality*, or the fact that they tend to involve, as James put it, "states of insight" which "seem to those who experience them to be also states of knowledge" (2002: 295). With respect to religious epistemology, then, two general types of inquiries arose: Some philosophers concerned themselves with whether subjects who held particular theistic beliefs on the basis of their own purportedly theophanic experiences could be justified (or otherwise warranted) in so doing, such that, if those beliefs were true, they would constitute religious knowledge. Other philosophers were more concerned with whether the fact of widespread reports of religious experience throughout recorded history could provide evidence for theism more generally and, if so, what the force of that evidence might be.

The attempts to answer one or both of these questions in the affirmative has tended to rely on the establishment of an *analogy* between certain forms of theophanic experience, on the one hand, and sense perception on the other. The majority of contemporary arguments for the epistemic value of religious experience has been developed on the basis of this comparison, though the arguments themselves differ widely, depending on the epistemological approach and the aims endorsed by their respective proponents. In this section, we will look at two prominent approaches to the "perceptual model" of religious experience that have driven many of these discussions.

3.1 Theophanic Experiences as Vehicles for Individual Justification

One approach proposed by champions of what has come to be known as *Reformed epistemology* employs a strong analogy between sense perception and theophanic experience to develop a "partners-in-crime" approach to the epistemology of religious experience. The general strategy is largely defensive, aimed at warding off religious skeptics and other critics of the epistemic value of religious experience by drawing parallels between cases in which a subject's beliefs about objects in the external world are grounded in their direct and unmediated sensory perception of those objects and those in which a subject's theistic beliefs are grounded immediately and noninferentially in putative perceptions of God. If it can be shown that the criticisms launched against the latter kind of belief can equally be applied to cases of the former, then, other things being equal, such experientially formed religious beliefs might be on no shakier epistemic ground than beliefs formed on the basis of sense perception. Given that we generally trust the deliverances of sense perception and take our sensory faculties to be reliable, despite encountering difficulty in accounting for the legitimacy of such belief-forming practices, proponents of this view aver that we should perhaps not be so quick to dismiss the deliverances of purported "religious perception" or the possibility that there could, for all we know, be such thing as a "God-detecting faculty" that operates on a spiritual level in a way similar to how our sense modalities operate on the physical level.

One of the most prominent advocates of this kind of strategy is William Alston. In his groundbreaking book *Perceiving God* (1993), he uses the term *mystical perception* to refer to cases in which subjects report "an experiential awareness of God," where "the awareness is direct and [. . .] reported to be of God" (14). Such experiences are claimed to immediately and noninferentially give rise to what Alston calls "M-beliefs," or "beliefs to the effect that God is doing something currently vis-à-vis the subject – comforting, strengthening, guiding, communicating a message, sustaining the subject in being – or to the effect that God has some (allegedly) perceivable property – goodness, power, lovingness" (1). Alvin Plantinga, too, puts forward an account that we might place in the "spiritual senses" tradition (cf. Abraham 2012), insofar as he develops a view according to which basic experiential theistic beliefs could arise through the operation of what he, following Calvin, calls the *sensus divinitatis*, or a "disposition [...] to form theistic beliefs in various circumstances, in response to the sorts of conditions or stimuli that trigger the working of this sense of divinity" (Plantinga 2000: 173).

In true Reidian fashion, neither Alston nor Plantinga is particularly interested in showing *de facto* that putative perceptions of God are veridical but rather, as Alston puts it, merely to "*rebut objections* to the conviction of the subjects that they are directly aware of God, and to point out that if their conviction is correct they are also properly taken to be *perceiving* God" (1993: 5). In other words, with respect to theophanic experience both thinkers are interested, first, in countering *de jure* objections that there is something "epistemically unacceptable," "foolish," "unjustified," "unreasonable," or otherwise "epistemically deplorable" in believing on the basis of such experience (Plantinga 2000: 3) and, second, in making room for the *possibility* that individual subjects who come to believe particular theistic propositions on the basis of direct, perception-like experiences of God could, absent defeaters, plausibly be said to be in possession of genuine religious *knowledge* should those beliefs turn out to be true. The idea is thus to show that experiential theistic beliefs could be *justified* (e.g., the product of a reliable, truth-conducive belief-forming process, as Alston would have it) or otherwise *warranted* (e.g., produced by properly functioning cognitive faculties in an appropriate environment for those faculties according to a "design plan" aimed successfully at truth, as Plantinga proposes). Plantinga's approach ultimately diverges from Alston's, but when it comes to defending the rationality of religious beliefs formed on the basis of purportedly nonsensory, perception-like experiences, he follows a not dissimilar line of reasoning. However, given the concerns Plantinga expresses regarding both the terms "perception" and "experience" (180ff.), together with the fact that he is less centrally concerned with religious experience as such, I will focus primarily on Alston's approach in what follows, as it has set the pattern for much of the analytic literature on the epistemology of religious experience. (For Alston's and Plantinga's discussions of each other, see Alston [1993]: 195ff., and Plantinga [2000]: 134ff.)

As noted above, Alston develops a "partners-in-crime" strategy with respect to sensory and theistic perception. He thereby attempts to show that what he calls "direct mystical perception" is a coherent notion analogous to, but importantly not identical with, sense perception. According to Alston's direct realist account of perception, or the "Theory of Appearing," the notion of some object's appearing perceptually to someone is "fundamental and unanalyzable," such that perceptions – whether sensory or mystical – have a "non- or preconceptual character" (1993: 55). Additionally, a subject's perceiving X necessarily involves X's figuring causally in the production of the experience in question. Alston does qualify that the concepts and background beliefs that the subject brings to the experience can influence the way X seems to them, but he does not think this involves their *conceptualizing* X in a certain way (39). This allows him to walk the tightrope between the common perennialist claim that religious experience is non- or preconceptual and the constructivist assertion that prior belief systems can affect or shape the character of a subject's experience. (Alston himself claims to remain agnostic with regard to this debate.)

Alston thinks his account of perception applies equally well to sense perception and to direct mystical perception, and he cites several experiential reports intended to provide historical examples of the Theory of Appearing at work in the latter (many of them unfortunately culled second-hand from James, Underhill, or other twentieth-century sources and taken largely out of context). He concludes that "a scrutiny of the reports of [theophanic] experiences reveals that the mode of consciousness involved is distinctively perceptual; it seems to the subject that something (identified by the subject as God) is directly presenting itself to his/her awareness as so-and-so." If this is right, and if God exists, then, he thinks, at least some of these experiences could amount to "a genuine perception of God" (Alston 1993: 67).

Alston then goes on to explore the justification (in the sense of the reliability or truth-conduciveness) of sense perception. Since he has claimed that perception is nonconceptual but can be informed by the perceiver's background beliefs, he needs to show how he can incorporate raw experience, interpretation, and cultural context into his account of the way perceptions produce reliable beliefs. To do so, he introduces the notion of a *doxastic practice*, or "the exercise of a system or constellation of belief-forming habits or mechanisms, each realizing a function that yields beliefs with a certain kind of content from inputs of a certain type" (Alston 1993: 155). He claims that both *sense-perceptual practice* (SP) and *mystical-perceptual practice* (MP) are of the "generational" sort, producing beliefs from nondoxastic inputs (104).

The problem for both SP and MP arises when it comes to successfully demonstrating that these doxastic practices are reliable in such a way that would (at least *prima facie*) justify the beliefs elicited through them. Alston spends much time showing the difficulty of establishing the reliability of SP without running into the problem of epistemic circularity, and he makes an extended effort to show that various attempts to solve this problem fail. Yet even if we cannot *show* it, he claims, we do not doubt that SP is generally reliable. In fact, he concludes that so long as we have no sufficient reason to regard a doxastic practice as *unreliable*, it is rational for a subject to engage in it – at least so long as it is "socially established," yields beliefs "free from massive internal and external contradiction," and "demonstrates a significant degree of self-support" (Alston 1993: 184). And Alston thinks SP clearly meets these requirements.

What does this mean for MP and the status of the theistic "M-beliefs" that are its output? To begin, Alston's defensive "partners-in-crime" strategy helps him with the common charge that MP is epistemically circular, insofar as all attempts to justify it rely in some way on theological presuppositions or other M-beliefs. For if SP, too, falls prey to this objection then it would appear to lose much of its force. Critics of the epistemic value of religious experience must either embrace an unattractive consequence concerning SP (e.g., radical skepticism, solipsism, or an external world radically different from that presented by the senses) or admit the possibility that the theistic beliefs of some religious subjects might likewise be *prima facie* justified by an appeal to mystical perception. Minimally, it means that MP cannot be considered *epistemically inferior* to SP, at least not on the grounds of circularity (Alston 1993: 143).

Indeed, with respect to specifically *Christian* mystical practice (CMP) – which takes "the Bible, the ecumenical councils of the undivided church, Christian experience through the ages, Christian thought, and more generally the Christian tradition as normative sources of its overrider system" (Alston 1993: 193) – if it cannot be decisively shown to be an *unreliable* doxastic practice, this allows that its outputs may be *prima facie* justified and thus at least represent candidates for religious knowledge. Of course, the justification for CMP will be internal to the practice itself. But relying on theological notions internal to the practice, it is claimed, is no more suspect than relying on sense perception to justify SP, at least absent any further reason to doubt the practice. In fact, Alston relies on the "partners-in-crime" strategy to maintain that CMP is at least in good company in its inability to fully address certain challenges to it.

Alston's approach provides one promising strategic variant for defending the potential epistemic value of religious experience, insofar as it makes room for the *situatedness* of experiential religious belief. That is, it recognizes the importance to religious perception of the individual's embeddedness in a doxastic practice or in theologically underpinned models of belief formation. As Harriet Harris puts it, it takes seriously the fact that "our social, psychological, physical or religious history enables us to become aware of things and to believe things that it is most unlikely someone without the same sets of experiences or situations would become aware of or believe" (2005: 109). And it recognizes the potential of these situated experiences to create opportunities for subjective religious learning and growth.

At the same time, it is also important to note both the limited and heavily conditional scope of tying theophanic experience to sense perception using the partners-in-crime approach. To be sure, if the analogy is a good one, this kind of approach can show that religious perception might be no more epistemically "guilty" than sense perception in certain respects. But this is a far cry from showing that either form of perception predictably and consistently yields veridical beliefs, and there may be independent reasons to think that Alston's CMP is unreliable. Moreover, as Harris points out, Reformed epistemology itself is a rather modest and *unambitious* epistemology. If the most we can expect from an epistemology of religious experience is a heavily conditional "license to believe" on the basis of experience or the tempered assurance that, absent defeaters, we are not doing anything "epistemically untoward" in so believing, we may wonder whether we really have an account of how religious experience can be genuinely epistemically *valuable* for the religious life in its various dimensions.

3.2 Theophanic Experiences as Evidence in Arguments for Theism

Whereas Reformed epistemology has traditionally been somewhat cynical regarding the ultimate promise of the natural theological enterprise with respect to demonstrating the existence and nature of God, some epistemologists have displayed more optimism about religious experience's ability to provide solid data for theistic arguments. In contrast to the preceding approach, which employs a largely defensive strategy to show that theophanic experience is, in certain crucial respects, no more epistemically "guilty" than the sense perception, *evidentialist* approaches to the epistemology of religious experience have traditionally traded on a more positive "partners in innocence" analogy. Two evidentialist accounts in this vein are those put forward by Richard Swinburne in *The Existence of God* (2004) and Caroline Franks Davis in *The Evidential Force of Religious Experience* (1989), both of whom have developed evidential arguments from theophanic experience as part of their larger cumulative cases for perfect-being theism more generally.

Both philosophers concede from the outset that, given its "private" and "subjective" nature, theophanic experience by itself is insufficient to demonstrate the probability of the theistic hypothesis over its atheistic alternatives.

However, as Franks Davis notes, even though certain arguments may be weak or easily defeated when taken individually, taken together in the context of a *cumulative case*, "the whole is greater than the sum of the parts," and the various parts can likewise provide mutual support to one another, "like the members of an athletic team" (1989: 109). Ultimately, both Swinburne and Franks Davis think that, once other arguments and sources of evidence have minimally demonstrated that theism is *not more improbable* than its counterparts, the evidence provided by theophanic experience might be sufficient to actually tip the scales in favor of the theistic hypothesis (Swinburne 2004: 341; Franks Davis 1989: 240). Franks Davis further argues that once the scale has been tipped, even those experiences that, taken alone, were initially rather weak from an evidential standpoint can come to play new, more significant evidential roles for relevantly situated religious subjects (245ff.).

The evidential argument concedes that theophanic experience is not universal to all epistemic subjects. Swinburne is remarkably adamant about this, and in various places he argues that if God's existence and plans were too obvious, human moral freedom would be severely compromised. Still, he thinks, we might nevertheless have good reason to expect that – if God did exist – God would show Godself to "some people, although perhaps not to everyone" (Swinburne 2004: 293). If this is so, then the question remains whether and how these "private and occasional" theophanies could have genuine evidential value for anyone other than those who are divinely favored enough to be on the receiving end of such manifestations. Given that Swinburne thinks that theophanic experiences are usually *private* perceptions, such that "when one person has a religious experience, his neighbour equally attentive and equally well equipped with sense organs and concepts normally does not" (297–298), he must show how such experiences can be evidence for anything beyond themselves and for anyone beyond those who have them.

Indeed, for evidentialists like Swinburne and Franks Davis, the challenge is to be able to make purportedly subjective, private experiences of God into something publicly accessible and "epistemically respectable" that can enter into discursive arguments for the existence of God (Coakley 2009). However, to transform private theophanic experiences of the Jamesian persuasion into publicly accessible events with evidential force, Swinburne and Franks Davis take a slightly different approach than that of Alston and Plantinga. Like the Reformed epistemologists, they begin with things we take to be true about sense perception to motivate the *prima facie* epistemic value of theophanic experiences, but they do so by emphasizing the idea that theophanic experience is a *species* of perceptual experience, such that any principle of rationality which applies to perception *tout court* will also apply to it. So if fundamental claims about the epistemic value of sense perception can plausibly be extended to *all* forms of perceptual experience, then by tying theophanic experience to such perception via analogy, or by nesting it under perception more generally, proponents of theism can perhaps provide religious experience with a more solid epistemological footing (Franks Davis 1989: 77).

This is exactly the tactic that Swinburne and Franks Davis adopt. Even though Swinburne takes the majority of theophanic experiences to be perceptions of a private and nonshared (perhaps even nonshare*able*) nature, he thinks that, *qua* perceptions, they are nevertheless subject to two epistemological principles – namely, the *Principle of Credulity* and the *Principle of Testimony*. The former maintains "that (in the absence of special considerations), if it seems (epistemically) to a subject that x is present (and has some characteristic), then probably x is present (and has that characteristic)" (Swinburne 2004: 303). Put a bit differently, although a subject's having a perceptual-like seeming of some object or state of affairs does not entail that the object or state of affairs actually exists or obtains, the subject's having had the experience provides at least *prima facie* evidence for the reality of its purported percept (Franks Davis 1989: 94). Of course, whereas the Principle of Credulity has largely to do with the subject's own justification for believing, a further principle is needed in order to bring private experiences into the public sphere. Swinburne's Principle of Testimony complements the Principle of Credulity by postulating that "the experiences of others are (probably) as they report them" – at least so long as we do not have good reason to think that they have misreported, misremembered, or misinterpreted their experiences (2004: 322).

Taken together, the Principles of Credulity and Testimony render both subjective perceptual beliefs and testimonial reports about perceptual experiences "innocent until proven guilty." This approach, Swinburne maintains, not only reflects the way we actually tend to proceed when trying to epistemically navigate the world, it is rationally *necessary* to avoid sinking into "a sceptical bog, in which we know hardly anything" (2004: 306). If this is correct, and the analogy between theophanic experience and sense perception is strong enough, then such religious experiences, too, must benefit from the presumption of epistemic innocence, placing the burden on the skeptic to provide defeaters for the evidential claim made by the religious subject on the basis of their experience.

By positioning religious experiences in such a way, Swinburne opens the door for a more ambitious epistemological approach: Not only does a particular instance of purported theophanic experience provide *prima facie* evidence for the beliefs the individual experiencer forms on the basis of their experience, but also – given that people's experiences are generally as they report them to be, together with the (according to Swinburne, indubitable) fact that "millions of human beings down the centuries" have reported experiences of this kind – theophanic experience may provide significant, though defeasible, evidence for the theistic hypothesis in general and can thus serve to bolster the cumulative case in favor of theism. In this way, then, appeals to religious experience can be used to do more than simply justify those who already believe; they can also be wielded against the skeptic in larger apologetic contexts and can play a decisive role in a larger argument-to-the-best-explanation for theism.

Of course, as William Abraham has pointed out, the Principles of Credulity and Testimony still represent a quite minimalistic approach to epistemology, since they claim nothing more than "that the mere appearing of p to be true gives initial ground for p being true" (2012: 280). And the cumulative arguments of Swinburne and Franks Davis will lose much of their strength if it can be shown that there are plausible defeaters for the majority of claims grounded in theophanic experience. Thus, for both Reformed epistemological and evidentialist approaches to religious experience, a lot hangs on the ability of the account in question to handle challenges to the analogy and alternative explanations of the experiences in question. It will thus be helpful to look at some of the most prominent objections that proponents of the perceptual model of religious experience must face to varying degrees, at least so long as they are interested in defending the general reasonableness of theistic belief on (at least partially) experiential grounds and the possibility that such belief, if true, could amount to genuine religious knowledge.

4 Challenges to the Perceptual Model

In each of the broader epistemological approaches to religious experience discussed in the last section, much of the success of the case for religious experience as a source of evidence or reasonable belief depends on the strength of the proposed relation between theophanic experience and sense perception. Where there appear to be relevant disanalogies between paradigm cases of theophanic experience and sensory experience, the onus would seem to be on the champion of the perceptual model of religious experience to explain how the kinds of theophanic experiences in which they are interested could be considered reliable or trustworthy in spite of these differences. We will examine four of these challenges here. (For a more thorough discussion of the various object-, description-, and subject-related challenges, see Franks Davis [1989]; Gale [1991]; Fales [1996a].)

4.1 Concerning God's Perceptibility

One significant worry when it comes to perceptual models of religious experience is that they are taken to involve the perception of something that is not only purported to be wholly spiritual but which is also supposed to transcend all human categories and capacities of apprehension – namely God. Some apophatic or negative theologians even go so far as to maintain that *nothing* can be positively said about the divine. Yet cognizable objects of perception tend to be entities of which we can positively predicate things or which present themselves as the bearers of (in principle) identifiable properties. So on strong apophatic views there appear to be three options: First, one could maintain that God is not perceivable at all. Second, one could maintain that God is perceivable but not positively cognizable or describable. Finally, one could claim that God is cognizable but that the very structure of the way we relate perceptually to God involves some sort of "disruption" or "overturning" of the ordinary perceptual situation (Yadav 2015). All three options present problems for the perceptual model, insofar as the model implicitly or explicitly maintains that the perceptual nature of theophanic experience is structurally more or less parallel to the way we relate to the ordinary objects of sense perception in the world around us.

At the same time, it is unclear whether more cataphatic models – at least those informed by a personalist approach to perfect-being monotheism – have an easier time making sense of exactly what theophanic perception is supposed to be. Such approaches allow that we *can* positively predicate certain features of God, features which we also predicate of human persons, such as goodness, knowledge, or power. God, however, is taken to have these properties to the greatest (possible) measure. And although philosophers disagree about whether to think of these properties as infinite or merely maximal, as well as whether they are predicated univocally or analogically of God and human beings, a genuine question arises about what it would mean for someone to have a *finite* perception of these kinds of *immeasurable* qualities. Calling this "the superlatives problem," Mark Webb notes that the monotheist "must have the conceptual resources to [perceptually] recognize an omnipotent being, and distinguish it from merely very powerful beings, and similarly for the other alleged divine attributes" (2015: 61). Yet one might think that, as John L. Mackie famously put it, "nothing in an experience as such could reveal a creator of the world, or omnipotence, or omniscience, or perfect goodness, or eternity, or even that there is just one god" (1982: 182).

Thus, regardless of whether we are talking about the "Divine Abyss" of negative theology or the "omni-God" of classical theism, the question arises as to whether God (and any features that might attach to that God) could even be the kind(s) of object that could be perceived by finite, embodied human beings like us. In fact, on either view, claiming that one has *perceived* God might even be theologically tantamount to *idolatry*, to reducing the nonperceivable divine to just another ordinary perceptible object and thus creating a false divine image – or, as Paul Tillich put it, to making God into merely "one being among others," such that the divine "ceases to be the God who is really God" (1973: 172).

Analytic philosophers of religion have not traditionally shown all that much sympathy for apophatic theology, nor in the apophatic modes of speech often employed by the mystics they so fondly cite (Coakley 2009). Neither do they deal extensively with the problems raised by negative theology for claims concerning theophanic experience. (An excellent exception is taken up in Yadav [2016].) With respect to the worries about cataphatic approaches, Alston admits that there are "limits of what God experientially presents [Godself] to us *as*" and that we should expect that the divine *rarely* presents itself as classical theology tends to describe it – that is, "as creator, three Persons in one Substance, the actor in salvation history, or even omnipotent, omniscient, and a se" (1993: 293). To arrive at these conclusions, he thinks, we will most likely need revelation or natural theology. Instead, Alston chooses to focus on experiences whose noetic aspect involves learning "what God is doing vis-à-vis oneself at the moment" or "what God's will is for oneself in particular," since these cannot be gleaned from the conclusions of scriptural revelation or rational proof. Swinburne, in contrast, focuses largely on experiences purporting to provide evidence of the omnipotent, omniscient, and a se nature of the God of classical theism, insinuating that it might actually be *easier* for some persons to recognize being in the presence of *unlimited* power, knowledge, and freedom than to perceptually detect finite instantiations of these properties in their fellow human beings. (The assumption seems to be that an object's having *more* of some property or feature makes it more readily recognizable.) Still, he admits that "*some* mild suspicion is cast on a subject's claim to have recognized an agent with these qualities by the qualitative remoteness of his previous experiences from what he claims to have detected" (Swinburne 2004: 319). Thus, whereas Alston is more concerned with the epistemic credibility of more specific, relational kinds of experiences in which one purportedly learns about God's particular relation to or action concerning oneself, Swinburne is concerned more with experiences of God *qua* "omni-God," claiming that the more specific, relational forms of theophanic experience emphasized by Alston have "lower evidential worth" for a cumulative argument for God's existence, even if they may prove to be of some indirect evidential value (325).

There is, however, a somewhat more nuanced version of the imperceptibility objection worth exploring in a bit more detail, if only because Alston and Plantinga both explicitly address a form of it. In *On the Nature and Existence of God* (1991), Richard Gale argues that it is *conceptually impossible* for there to be a genuine, veridical perception of God. Gale's overall project is to show that the disanalogies between sense perception and theophanic experience are significant enough to undermine the kinds of analogical arguments being made in favor of their epistemic value, whether of the "partners-in-crime" or the "partners-in-innocence" variety. He argues that for a sense perception to be veridical, it must be possible for its object to be the "common object of different sense perceptions," which in turn requires that it is "housed in a space and time that includes both the object and perceiver" (326–327). However, on most common understandings of what God is or could be, it would seem that God, being outside space and time, could not be the object of an immediate *sensory* perception. But what about nonsensory perceptions? If this were possible, Gale thinks, there would have to be some sort of further analogous dimension(s) of objective existence that both God and the religious perceiver could plausibly inhabit that "can be invoked to make sense of God existing when not actually perceived and being the common object of different religious experiences" (327). Yet it is unclear what such an "analogous dimension" might be. Although Gale allows that there might be nonspatiotemporal realities, such as Platonic Ideas or realms, he thinks it impossible to *perceive* those realities, even if we can come to know about them in other ways. Hence he thinks the idea of God is "categorially unsuited to be the object of a veridical perception, whether it be of a sensory or nonsensory kind" (327).

How can the defender of the perceptual model respond? Alston is a bit cagey on this matter, but he writes in a footnote that he is "inclined to think that what we know about sense perception provides a strong empirical argument against the possibility for God's directly appearing to *sensory* experience" (1993: 59 n. 49). However, with regard to nonsensory experience, he sees no reason to suppose that, if God exists, God could bring it about *supernaturally* that someone has an experience of God without requiring that we understand the mechanism by which such an experience is elicited. Plantinga, too, sees no good reason why God could not present Godself to human beings in a nonsensory fashion (e.g., via the *sensus divinitatis*) and maintains that Gale's objection rests on a failure to recognize that, in order to identify their perceptions at different times as perceptions of the same God, subjects need only form the true belief under warrant-conferring conditions that they encountered God on these occasions (2000: 342). Of course, both Alston's and Plantinga's responses merely make room for the possibility that, *if* God exists, persons *might* be able to perceive God. But this will likely be of little consolation to the critic, especially insofar as the question of the existence of God is precisely what is under discussion.

A more promising approach might make reference to the fact that sensory experiences themselves sometimes pick out features that do not really describe the physical object of perception itself. Quite often, in fact, the way things seem to us in perception are not exactly the way things "really" are. (Consider, for example, those who maintain that colors are not features of the objects themselves.) Yet even these seemings can be epistemically valuable by helping us to better hone in on particular objects, or to make distinctions between them, or to learn about what they might be like in some other respect. Likewise, we tend to think that some experiences of a physical or bodily nature assist us in picking out or "perceiving" nonphysical facts or facts of a very different kind – as when, for example, affective somatic experiences help us pick out morally or aesthetically salient features of a situation. In a similar fashion, indirect, *materially mediated* religious experiences that either literally or symbolically "point beyond themselves" might hold more promise for addressing the worry about God's imperceptibility, since they do not require perception of God to be direct and could even potentially make room for the negative claims of apophatic theology. I take up this kind of approach in more detail in the final section.

Additionally, some "alternative" accounts of theism may be better able to counter the perceptibility worry. For example, some pan(en)theist approaches consider the physical universe to be coextensive with (or, minimally, part of) God (Buckareff and Nagasawa 2016); other views suggest that the world constitutes God's "body" (cf. Jantzen 1984; McFague 1993; Mawson 2006). On such views, to perceive the world with our senses *just is* to perceive God (or a part of God, or some aspect of God). This, then, would allow for a conception of God on which perception could be genuinely *direct*, and for which no analogy between sense perception and theophanic experience would be necessary.

4.2 Concerning Checkability Criteria

Whereas the perceptibility challenge largely has to do with worries concerning the very possibility of perceptual-like theophanic experience, one might also worry about its purported status as a form of *cognitive* experience (one capable of yielding religious *knowledge*) if it cannot be reliably checked, corroborated, or otherwise tested for veridicality. In the realm of sense perception, there exist more-or-less universally accepted cross-checking procedures to distinguish between genuine and delusory/illusory experiences or to decide between hypotheses. For example, we often ask people who are similarly situated and perceptually competent whether they report having a similar experience. Or we seek corroboration for the perception of one sense modality via other sense modalities – or by using technical equipment. We consider whether the subject's claim is consistent with our relevant background knowledge, and we test and accordingly modify, retest, and remodify auxiliary assumptions, auxiliaries of auxiliaries, and so on. We can check whether predictions made on the basis of the experience come to genuine fruition and are repeatable. We may even ask about the reporting subject's physiological and psychological state, their overall competence, their honesty and consistency, and so on. (For similar lists, see Wainwright [1973]; Franks Davis [1989: 71]; Gale [1991: 302]; Fales [1996a: 27ff].)

However, in the case of theophanic experience, it is hard to see how the large majority of experiences under discussion by proponents of the nonsensory perceptual model of theophanic experience could be checked in ways analogous to the empirical tests for sense perceptions – especially if they really are, as many philosophers take them to be, private and privileged, not generally shared, repeatable, or accessible to others or "the sort of thing which can easily be produced for observation in a controlled setting" (Franks Davis 1989: 115). Still, if we take the partners-in-crime assumption about the circularity involved in the justification of both MP and SP, together with the partners-in-innocence claim that beliefs or assertions based on perceptual experiences are innocent until proven guilty, we may be inclined to conclude that the disanalogies between the checks and tests for theophanic experience and those for sense perception are not so threatening as to undermine the analogy altogether.

Indeed, Alston thinks the comparison between SP and MP can be maintained, despite the above disanalogies. He concedes that having an "overrider system" is how we normally get from mere *prima facie* justification to all-out justification. Moreover, he considers having a checking system like that we employ for sense perception an "epistemic desideratum" for any doxastic practice, including mystical perception (Alston 1993: 220, see also 189ff.). He also admits that the varieties of SP have one more-or-less overarching overrider system, whereas MP's overrider system is always indexed to the particular tradition within which it is situated. But this dissimilarity, he claims, "does not negate the fact that each form of MP does have a working overrider system" based on its particular credal and doctrinal context (211). These kinds of overrider systems are legitimate, he claims, even if the checking procedures assume certain theological truths from the get-go, since SP, as we have seen, is equally unable to produce tests for genuineness that do not themselves rely on sense perception. Moreover, he doubles down on his partners-in-crime strategy by suggesting that even sense perception does not necessarily enjoy the kind of uniformity we often suppose of it, such that our checking procedures for SP may be less reliable than we are inclined to think.

So what kinds of checks or overriders can there be on theophanic experience that would point to its acceptability as a potentially reliable way of forming beliefs? Franks Davis lists four checking procedures for Christian mystical practice (CMP): (i) the experiences display internal and external consistency, (ii) they bear predictable moral and spiritual fruits, (iii) they are consistent with orthodox doctrine, and (iv) the subject is psychologically and mentally competent (1989: 71ff.). William Wainwright lists similar criteria, with the additional claim that (v) "the depth, the profundity and the 'sweetness' of what the mystic says on the basis of his experience counts in favor of the genuineness of that experience [whereas] the silliness of what he says counts against it" (1973: 261). To the charge that such checks rely on a theological underpinning that begs the question in favor of the reliability of such experiences, Franks Davis claims that criteria (i) and (iv) do not actually presuppose any particular theological or doctrinal background, and that (ii) and (v) do not even require theological belief. She concedes that (iii) does involve circularity insofar as it is indexed to the doctrine in question, but claims that it nonetheless still allows for a "great diversity of experiences" to fall within its scope (Franks Davis 1989: 73–74).

However, this response might be too hasty. To begin, it is not entirely plausible that criteria (i), (ii), (iv), and (v) are as "theologically innocent" as Franks Davis proposes. With respect to internal and external consistency (i), it is unclear whether the various mystical experiences reported even within a very specific timeframe in the context of a particular tradition or doxastic practice produce experiences that entail consistent propositions about God. For example, although they are often placed within the same late medieval Christian mystical tradition, and although straightforward lines of influence can be traced between them, it is by no means clear that the ways Mechthild of Magdeburg, Marguerite Porete, Meister Eckhart, and Henry Suso speak about the nature of the soul's union with the divine are consistent. But demarcating a distinct MP anywhere we find inconsistencies not only begs the question, it also threatens to collapse into a problematic kind of "mystical relativism." Additionally, many reports of mystical experiences explicitly employ paradoxes or self-contradictory language, and while this may sometimes be strategic – e.g., using paradoxical language to gesture at the transcendent and ultimately incomprehensible nature of God – the evaluation of these "assertions" as consistent or inconsistent in light of such practical or performative ends requires, *pace* Franks Davis, the application of a particular theological framework. If such statements are "really" comprehensible (e.g., by virtue of what they *do*, not what they *say*), it will only be against a particular religious and cultural backdrop that informs their functions in these contexts. Finally, whether different belief outputs of the "same" religious doxastic practice are consistent with one another will likely involve a judgment from within the practice itself and will depend on that particular system's own tolerance for inconsistency.

Nor can the evaluations involved in (ii), (iv), and (v) be decided independently of the religious culture or doctrine in question. Criterion (ii), for example, depends on knowing what can count as "moral" or "spiritual" within the relevant religious tradition, so that the "fruits" of religious experience could be recognized as such. Moreover, with respect to (iv), what will count as "mental or physical competence" to perceive God religiously may differ radically from what counts as competence to perceive ordinary objects via the senses. The distrust of mental illness, intoxication, and "altered states" in our sensorial practices does not always hold for religious contexts, as we see in traditions where "holy madness," the ingestion of certain psychoactive substances, or states of "spiritual frenzy" are considered particularly conducive to veridical religious experience (cf., e.g., Dols 1992; Lipsedge 1996; Shanon 2002; Heriot-Maitland 2008). Finally, concerning (v), quality claims like "depth," "profundity," and "silliness" are themselves value-laden and involve not only an assessment of what is being said but also a consideration of who is *authorized* to make such assessments within the doxastic practice, which again is determined by religious and cultural context – and not seldomly in ways that marginalize certain groups or individuals according to religious in-group/out-group norms and other more general religious and cultural practices of exclusion (e.g., discrimination on the basis of gender, race, ability, class, etc.). Yet, as Jerome Gellman (2010) observes, if the overrider system of CMP (or some subtradition within it) can be shown to rest on mistaken physiological theories, or if they exhibit a tendency to marginalize women or other groups (e.g., in order to impose ecclesiastical order and preserve worldly structures of power), then we might have reason to worry about the truth conduciveness of the overrider system in question.

These worries are perhaps not particularly troubling to the defenders of nonsensory religious perception, so long as they are content with the partners-in-crime strategy. Indeed, what I have described above may just represent one more way of thinking about Alston's doxastic-practice approach, and questions can be raised as to whether SP, too, falls prey to many of these problems. At the same time, it is unclear whether the defenders of religious perceptual practice are not trying to have their cake and eat it too. If the defender of the epistemic value of theophanic experience consistently resorts to charges of double standards and epistemic imperialism on the part of the critic, there arises a certain tension, as Gale notes, between the "demands, on the one hand, for parity of treatment of the religious- and sense-experience doxastic practices and, on the other, that we not [. . .] uphold the epistemological principles of one practice as a standard by which to judge the adequacy of others" (1991: 321). In fact, although the onus is now claimed to be on the religious skeptic to make the case for religious perception's unreliability, it is unclear how it would ever be possible to meet the demands of this responsibility, short of either finding a knock-down-drag-out argument for atheism or undermining the reliability of a sufficient number of individual experiences using the epistemic standards of some relevant and established "meta-practice" shared by both the believer and the skeptic. But this seems unlikely to be forthcoming so long as the former refuses to allow the relevant standards of SP to apply to MP.

Evan Fales complicates the theist's case even further. He claims that a necessary condition of *any* doxastic practice claiming to produce justified perceptual beliefs about extramental objects involves being able to paint a causal picture that links the experience to its object in the right way: "Without *some* practical conception of the ways in which an item can causally influence us, we have no grounds for justifying the claim that one set of circumstances produces veridical perception, whereas another leads to error" (Fales 1996a: 28). And although Fales rightly thinks that most religious traditions have very good ideas of the *mundane* stimulus conditions for theophanic experience, he is concerned that mystical doxastic practices are unable to make an independently confirmable link to the *supramundane* side of the causal story and are thus unable to distinguish genuine from nongenuine experiences of God. If this is so, Fales thinks, then such doxastic practices can't be said to be *perceptual* practices, since the latter do not meet a necessary corollary of the causal condition on perception, namely being able "to establish suitable causal connections between object and subject" (36). Unlike Gale, Fales does not think such an account *cannot* be given, but he insists that some account "must *be* given before CMP can be taken seriously," placing the burden squarely back on the theist to provide a satisfactory account of the supernatural story that stands up satisfactorily to alternative explanations.

In the end, the force of the checkability challenge will depend on how significantly the doxastic practices associated with religious experience are taken to differ from that of sense perception and how heavily the proponent of the perceptual model relies on stories about supernatural causality to make their case for the rationality of experiential theistic belief. The Reformed epistemologist must be satisfied with tying checkability and overrider practices to the particular religious or doctrinal system in question, which in turn threatens to lead to a radical relativism concerning the epistemic appropriateness of theistic experiential belief. Evidentialists like Swinburne and Franks Davis, on the other hand, may be less concerned about checkability, so long as it does not significantly weaken their overall cumulative argument. Still, even here it raises serious questions about the ability of theophanic experience to decide the matter if the evidence for and against theism is a wash.

4.3 Competing Naturalist Claims

A further, equally pressing concern regarding the perceptual model of religious experience involves the worry that theophanic experience can be reduced to some naturalistic explanation or constellation of naturalistic explanations without loss of explanatory power. Justin Barrett (2007), for example, presents three plausible "biopsychological" approaches that aim to undermine the epistemic status of theistic beliefs formed or maintained on the basis of theophanic experience, even if they do not necessarily challenge the truth of theism itself. (That is, they yield forms of what Gellman [2001] calls "evidence-reductionism," as opposed to "truth-reductionism.") First, some *neurotheological* approaches claim that evolutionarily advantageous features of the brain have developed over time that also happen to generate illusory religious experiences of a theophanic nature. Second, the *group selection* approach claims that religious systems (and the experiences cultivated within them) encourage prosocial behavior, allowing them to "out-survive" non-prosocial systems and reproduce more easily. Finally, some approaches from within the *cognitive science of religion* (CSR) endorse a kind of perennialism about human conceptual structures, arguing that "in general, the basic functional processes of human minds are the same regardless of cultural environments," and that the "highly specialized conglomerates of many functional subsystems," which developed to solve very particular problems, "inform and constrain recurrent patterns of human thought and action including religious thought and action" (Barrett 2007: 59).

CSR theories in particular plausibly appeal to conceptual structures to reductively explain "recurrent features" of religion – including experiential belief in a God or gods. The so-called *HADD*, or "hypersensitive agency detection device," is maintained to be just such a structure. The HADD, it is claimed, causes subjects to interpret situations with relatively ambiguous evidence as involving some form of agency, since possessing a cognitive system yielding false positives would clearly exercise an advantage over those yielding a significant number of false negatives, when it came to the survival of our ancestors in the wild (Guthrie 1993). Barrett combines the HADD hypothesis with additional research led by Deborah Keleman on what she calls "promiscuous teleology," which concludes that children (and some adults under particular conditions) intuitively look for purpose or design in natural events (Kelemen 2004; Kelemen and Rosset 2009). Taken together, Barrett thinks, these two strands of CSR research give us good reason to believe that "humans have a natural, intuitive impetus for postulating gods" (2011: 102), which might give us a potentially strong reductionist explanation for theophanic experience that could undermine the rationality of experiential theistic belief. (For an alternative approach to HADD and the relationship of religious experience to religious belief, see van Leuuwen and Elk's [2019] "Interactive Religious Experience Model," or IREM. For an reductionist approach from a non-biopsychological direction, see Fales' sociological critique [1996b, 1996c, 1999] and Gellman's replies [1998, 2001].)

Most defenders of the epistemic value of the perceptual model agree with their opponents that if we have no good reason to think that God played any relevant causal role in a theophanic experience, then we have no business concluding that the experience was veridical. Hence, the most common strategies for countering challenges of the above kind are to challenge one or both of the following premises: (1) that a particular biopsychological explanation represents the *best* explanation for theophanic experiences of the kind proposed by the perceptual model, and (2) that the biopsychological account in question gives us good reason to believe that theophanic experiences are *not* caused by anything supernatural (van Eyghen 2020).

Michael Murray, for example, has provided arguments that focus primarily on the second premise. With respect to (2) Murray argues that, as an agency-detecting mechanism, HADD is generally reliable, even though it misfires on occasion. Yet until we can show that HADD is more likely than not to be *unreliable* in the cases in which it identifies deities as the causes of certain experiences, we have not shown that its workings make experiential belief in God irrational or unjustified. Even if HADD does provide the best explanation for theophanic experience, it leaves space for God to play a causal role in the generation of such experience. It is even possible that "God set up our environment and the course of evolutionary history in such a way that we come to have cognitive tools that lead us to form beliefs in a supernatural reality" (Murray 2008: 368).

With regard to premise (1), Hans van Eyghen (2020) has argued that although certain biopsychological explanations might offer the best explanation for *some* theophanic experiences, they certainly cannot do so for *all* such experiences. Similarly, Jerome Gellman (2001) notes that there is a great diversity in theophanic experiences, and while the probability of the reliability of some particular type of theophanic experience may be reduced by recourse to a particular reductionist explanation, it is unclear whether any (set of) naturalistic explanations could sufficiently undermine the evidential force of *all* forms of such experience. He notes that many theorists make the mistake of focusing solely on mystical experience of a "more dramatic and bizarre" nature, while

overlooking the wide preponderance of "normal," "everyday" mystical episodes among many religious persons that do not fit the mold of the kinds of
experiences being explained away by reductionist accounts (93). However, as
we shall see in the next section, this very diversity of theophanic experiences
presents a further problem for the theistic defender of the perceptual model.

In the end, although little progress has been made in these and similar debates
between those defending theism and the rationality of religious belief and those
hoping to debunk religious belief via naturalistic explanation, there is still room
for increased engagement of a less hostile sort, especially since this area of
discourse represents one of the key intersections of religious epistemology with
empirical research being conducted on religious experience and belief in the
natural and social sciences. As Wesley J. Wildman has pointed out, Alston and
many other proponents of the perceptual model have to a large degree moved so
quickly from the causal level of description of religious experience to the
doxastic level in their attempts to defend theistic belief that they have failed
to "take proper account of the neurological and evolutionary conditioning of
human cognitive activity" (2011: 164). Yet doing so might help them bolster
their case, as opposed to undermining it. On the flip side of this coin, empirical
researchers would do well to work with philosophers to help make the concepts
that drive their studies more precise and commensurable with research across
disciplinary lines. However, productive dialogues of these kinds are still too few
and far between. Hence, this debate can be taken as an impetus for future
collaborations between philosophers, theologians, and members of the empirical disciplines, especially if philosophers of religion really want to uphold the
analogy between sensory and religious cognition.

Additionally, it might be possible to take an empirical approach to theophanic
experience that is *nonreductive* in nature, as Kenneth Pargament (2013a, 2013b)
claims. Instead of reducing spirituality to some more basic explanatory level,
Pargament argues that there are good theoretical, practical, and empirical
reasons for treating it as a distinct motivation and process that can stand
alongside other (e.g., psychological, social, physiological) levels of analysis.
Since "a substantial portion of the world's population looks at life through
a sacred lens [. . .] that colors, filters, and clarifies their view of reality," and
given the possibility that religion and spirituality may represent "dimensions of
life that [are] at least partially responsible for our distinctiveness as human
beings," Pargament thinks that a wholly reductionist empirical approach is
likely both to misunderstand those who occupy a religious or spiritual perspective and to simply miss interesting and important aspects of the human experience (2013a: 269). Such an approach, then, may be more likely to take
experiential reports by religious subjects more seriously. This, too, may open

up new avenues for cooperation between the empirical sciences and philosophy of religion, even if it does little to resolve the debate between theists and atheists.

4.4 Competing Religious Claims

In §4.3, we looked at competing claims coming from the largely secular camp, which employs naturalistic explanations for religious experience as a way of undermining the epistemic value of the perceptual model. One way of responding to this worry involves invoking the diversity of types of theophanic experiences amongst and within the various religious traditions. However, even if this sort of appeal to a diversity in *kind* can perhaps counter the reductionist challenge, there is also the problem of diversity in *content* – that is, of the competing claims to religious knowledge that arise out of the experiences of adherents of different religious traditions or subtraditions. As Franks Davis notes, if "subjects cannot agree on a description of the alleged percept, their experiences must be at worst, illusory, at best, serious misperceptions, and in any case, generally unreliable" (1989: 166). If this is right, then the secular challenge may, via an appeal to diversity in content, gain back some of the tenability it lost through the appeal to diversity in kind.

Quite obviously, religious disagreement on the basis of experience can arise between members of different religions. For example, a Christian might have an experience which they take to point to God's triune nature, whereas a Muslim may argue on the basis of their experience that God is wholly one and unified, while a Santerían may argue for polytheism on the basis of their experiences of a panoply of gods. This, of course, is in addition to the fact that not all religious experience is theophanic in nature, and the presence of religious traditions within which religious experience is largely nontheistic (e.g., as in certain strands of Buddhism) may also lead to incompatible beliefs between religious theists and religious nontheists.

The problem of diversity in content is not lost on proponents of the perceptual model. Since there is a significant amount of agreement with respect to the everyday objects of sense perception, if religious experience leads to radical religious disagreement this might yet again threaten the very analogy on which the perceptual model rests. Philosophers of religion tend to be very selective about the experiences they select as paradigm cases of theophanic experience, and like their naturalist counterparts they tend to focus on bizarre and dramatic episodes at the expense of more commonplace religious experiences. Yet, when faced with the problem of religious diversity, many philosophers retreat to a form of what Franks Davis calls "broad theism," or otherwise to a much vaguer form of perennialism than their paradigm cases might support. Some of these scholars, like John Hick (as we saw above), acknowledge religious diversity on the level of experience and interpretation but claim that ultimately all relevant experiences are, in fact, manifestations of some singular "ultimate reality." (Not everyone puts forward a two-worlds view like Hick, but the parable of the blind men and the elephant is never very far out of reach.) On views like this, differences in the content of religious experience are merely superficial – nothing more than retrospective interpretations informed by social and cultural context. But they all ultimately have as their "actual" object the same entity, being, or reality.

One potentially unfortunate consequence of this approach, however, is that it uncharitably implies that most (or even all) reports of religious experiences involve some misdescription, misinterpretation, or other shortcoming on the part of the experiencing subject. And in so doing, this strategy might also threaten to erase or trivialize significant religious and cultural differences that contribute in important ways to individual and group identity and ways of knowing. Failing to take these differences seriously, even if they really are superficial, is likely to result in a corresponding failure to address the ways in which actual religious encounter and conflict goes beyond the merely doxastic. Indeed, it is unclear whether simply clearing up semantic differences and reducing religious perspectives to one another is likely to result in more productive interfaith cooperation than sincerely admitting the diversity and distinctness of religious traditions. Granted, philosophical proponents of the perceptual model are usually more interested in defending the rationality of particular religious believers than resolving global religious conflict, but one may always ask about the potential perlocutionary effects of a certain form of discourse and what exactly we are trying to achieve with such a view. At what practical and epistemic cost is one prepared to defend the rationality of individual religious believers? What is ultimately won by focusing on religious believers in such a way?

Franks Davis herself presents a somewhat more nuanced view by claiming that, at a "very low degree of ramification" we can, in fact, locate a sort of "common core" of experiential claims that will cover most numinous and mystical experiences, but she is careful to emphasize that this is not to be understood as pushing for a kind of "universal religion." Still, she admits that reconciling conflicts at the level of highly ramified descriptions of religious experiences will require independent support beyond the experiences themselves, which is why she thinks we need independent and/or cumulative arguments to establish their evidential value (Franks Davis 1989: 175). Alston, too, is keen to push a more pluralistic view of religious experience, one which rests on the fact that there is a plurality of distinct (and, to some extent, mutually exclusive) mystical doxastic practices. In fact, he notes that on his doxastic-practice account there will have to be as many different MPs as there are different religions, doctrinal systems, or "conceptual schemes for grasping Ultimate Reality" (Alston 1993: 189, 192). He appears to be in agreement with Franks Davis that an independent argument would be required to finally settle disagreements arising between MPs, but he is less confident that arguments of this kind are forthcoming. Although he admits that in some instances a case could reasonably be made that one tradition's doxastic practice is epistemically superior to another, in other instances there might be no non-question-begging reason independent of the doxastic practices themselves to epistemically prefer one over the other. (In an interesting twist on the former possibility, Mark Webb [2015] uses Alston's doxastic-practice approach to argue that it is more rational to accept Theravada Buddhist experience claims than Christian ones.)

However, instead of giving up or significantly reducing confidence in our own particular MP in the face of religious diversity, Alston claims that so long as we have no *external* reason to think that competing MPs are more truth-conducive than our own, "the only rational course" is for us to "sit tight with the practice of which [we are] master and which serves [us] so well in guiding [our] activity in the world" (1993: 274). It is, however, questionable whether "sticking to one's doxastic guns" is the *only* rational course for someone considering the problem of experiential religious disagreement. Conversion is also clearly an option, unless already having "mastered" a doxastic practice versus learning a new one has clear epistemic or existential advantages, which might not always be the case. Where things are, epistemically speaking, a wash, all sorts of nonepistemic factors – such as aesthetic preference, preference of community, proximity to or social status of the tradition in question, or other pragmatic issues – may legitimately play a crucial role in one's decision. Moreover, as Phillip Quinn has pointed out, the choice is also not merely a binary stay-or-switch one. Another live option is the possibility of ceasing to engage in mystical doxastic practice altogether, or attempting to revise one's own practice from within "in ways that would improve its reliability if some refined pluralistic hypothesis were true" (Quinn 1995: 162). Quinn suggests that it may thus be equally rational for more pluralistically minded religious believers in a modern world to "move in the direction of thicker phenomenologies and thinner theologies" (163) – though this, too, may push for movement in a direction that erases rather than embraces difference, as we saw above.

The situation is further complicated when we remind ourselves that the problem here is not just one of *inter*religious disagreement. Religions are not monoliths, and when we really begin to take seriously the radical *intra*religious dynamism and diversity of religious traditions – e.g., in terms of subtraditions and sects, "marginal" versus "mainstream" movements, geographic location, ethnic and racial makeup, economic background, and so on – we find here, too, reports of radically different religious experiences yielding similarly incompatible beliefs about the object(s) of perception. Alston unfortunately presents a rather vague notion of "Christian Mystical Practice" (CMP) for his purposes, which takes as its overrider system "the Bible, the ecumenical councils of the undivided church, Christian experience through the ages, Christian thought, and more generally the Christian tradition" and "does not alter their traditional significance to such an extent as to make a mockery of them" (1993: 193). Alston is aware that this is not a very precise designation, but he claims that "if we try to precise the concept too much we end up with an unmanageable plurality of practices" and then moves on.

Yet within the confines of this imprecise designation, we find significant differences in experience that can and do lead to radically different beliefs about the nature of God. Moreover, as Kelli Potter (2013) notes, we cannot begin to deal with the problem of interreligious disagreement until we have an idea of how orthodoxy within the various religious traditions is to be demarcated. However, given what she calls "the problem of heterodoxy," it is unclear that we can even get started on this latter task, especially if she is right that the existence of persistent "ambiguous competent interpretative disagreements" gives us good reason to think that there is a genuine and irresolvable epistemic and semantic ambiguity when it comes to determining what counts as orthodox within some particular tradition. "*What divides us most deeply*," she writes, "*cuts across religious traditions rather than between them*" (Potter forthcoming).

Interestingly, Potter thinks this problem of the indeterminacy of orthodoxy results not from a lack of evidence, but rather from an *overabundance* of it. And for this reason, "appealing to religious experience doesn't help with the problem of internal religious disagreement; it exacerbates it" (Potter forthcoming). The problem is that using religious experience to settle one side of the disagreement, as Alston might have it, is a strategy equally available to the other side, giving both sides some claim to being the "real deal." However, if we are not even able to determine orthodoxy, then we also lose one of Alston's main checking procedures for the legitimacy of a theophanic experience from within any particular doxastic practice. That is, it is unclear what would qualify, in Alston's terms, as a mystical doxastic practice not relevantly deviating from or "making a mockery" of its overrider system. It is not clear that we could even get a full grasp on what the overrider system itself is without importing a large number of pragmatic, aesthetic, political, and social (i.e., *nonepistemic*) considerations into our deliberations. And most likely this is exactly what usually happens. As Potter puts it: "Religious agreement is often just pseudo-agreement. If someone tells you that she is a Christian, this doesn't really say as much about her beliefs or values as do her demographics."

Potter's approach leaves us with a deep skeptical problem, especially for religious epistemologies that want to use theophanic experience to undergird theistic claims. Of course, to draw once again on the analogy between sense perception and religious experience, we may want to bracket skeptical worries about religious orthodoxy, just as we bracket skepticism about the external world. Yet such a bracketing goes beyond purely epistemic considerations into the realm of the pragmatic, a consequence unpalatable to some religious epistemologists. Moreover, whereas there is an overwhelming amount of general agreement in belief among ordinary sense perceivers about the objects of sense perception, it is unclear whether there is enough general doxastic agreement among competent religious believers to license such a bracketing. Ultimately, even if one does not want to go as far as Potter does, the problem of heterodoxy among competent believers represent a serious threat to the epistemic value of experientially formed or maintained religious belief, one that must be taken seriously.

4.5 How Epistemically Valuable Are Religious Experiences Really?

The challenges discussed in this section raise serious concerns about the role that theophanic experiences can play in justifying theistic belief, at least insofar as the experiences in question are evaluated according to the perceptual model. Defenders of this model are often forced to either (a) radically downplay the differences in particular traditions and appeal to a broader and much less highly ramified version of theism, or (b) build increasingly specific theological content into their accounts, using a particular tradition to provide the contours of what counts as acceptable or legitimate experience. With (a), we might be left with a rather bland form of "generic theism" which erases important religious distinctions that make a genuine difference to religious adherents, both epistemically and practically. With (b), we might worry that such "theological bolstering" begs the question against both the atheist and members of all competing traditions, such that claims to objective knowledge are sufficiently weakened if not wholly undermined. In both cases, the religious epistemologist may have to be satisfied with the very limited conclusion that *if* some particular form of theism is true, then *some* experientially based religious beliefs *might* amount to religious knowledge. Is this all, then, that we can say for the epistemic value of religious experience?

I think not. But in order to adequately explore the epistemic (and social-practical) value of religious experience, we will need to expand both our epistemologies and the category of religious experience itself. In the final section, then, I will briefly survey a few ways that philosophy of religion can fruitfully undertake both of these tasks, as well as how it can better address how the epistemic, the practical, and the sociopolitical are intertwined in this domain. This will allow us to recognize the value of religious experience to the religious life more generally while at the same time taking the epistemic aspects of religious particularity and difference more seriously.

5 Expanding Experience

While both of the broad epistemological approaches discussed in Sections 3 and 4 are keen to draw parallels with sense perception in their discussions of the epistemological value of religious experience, they nevertheless tend to privilege *nonsensory* experiences over sensory or somatic ones. For example, although Alston admits that "not all mystical perception is devoid of sensory content," he goes on to assert that "it seems clear that a non-sensory appearance of a purely spiritual deity has a greater chance of presenting [it] as [it really] is than any sensory presentation" and that it "gives us a better chance of grasping what God is like in [Godself] than does any sensory experience" (1993: 18–20). Yet that this should be so, even if God is a "purely spiritual" being, is far from obvious (as is Alston's concomitant claim that, within the Christian context, the physical senses are capable of perceiving only Christ's human nature). Swinburne, too, notes parenthetically that he is speaking of awareness of God as a form of perception "without implying that the awareness is necessarily mediated via the normal senses" (2004: 296). And insofar as he goes on to privilege private, nonsharable theophanic experiences as paradigm cases, it quickly becomes apparent how prominent a place nonsensory religious experience occupies in his epistemological project.

Although most philosophers of religion will readily admit that religious experiences can take many forms, including sensory ones, the overwhelming amount of ink spilled on nonsensory-yet-quasi-perceptual, Jamesian-style, theistic experience far outweighs that discussing religious experience in any other sense. And it would not be surprising if someone coming to this literature for the first time might be given over to a kind of "implicit perennialism," or at least led to think that such experiences are the only kinds of religious experience of any real epistemic value. Yet it is far from clear that this should be so. Indeed, the rather myopic focus in philosophy of religion on nonsensual, theophanic perception likely arises in part from the longstanding tradition in Western European Christendom of regarding visions, auditions, and other bodily experiences with theological suspicion – a tradition with an extensive gendered, racialized, and colonialist history. Given this bias against the body, as well as the objections to the nonsensory, direct-perception model raised in Section 4, there might be good reason to widen the discourse on religious experience in the discipline and to examine alternative approaches.

5.1 Materially Mediated Religious Experience and the Expansion of Religious Epistemology

Insofar as many of the challenges to the perceptual model arise from purported disanalogies between nonsensory theophanic experience and sense perception, an account that relies on literal sense perception, as opposed to nonsensory perception or the perception of the so-called "spiritual senses," might have a better chance of avoiding these worries. One epistemological approach that focuses more closely on bodily religious experience of this kind places significant emphasis on the role of *mediated* or *indirect* perception of the divine, rather than on those experiences taken to be direct and immediate. This kind of approach was most prominently brought to attention in analytic circles by George Mavrodes (1970), but it has been taken up more recently by philosophers like David Brown (2004), C. Stephan Evans (2010, 2011), and Mark Wynn (2012, 2013). (Plantinga [2000], too, allows that religious beliefs may arise from sensory experience, though he skirts the question of whether warrant for these beliefs comes by way of the senses.)

Of course, there is a rather trivial sense in which *all* numinous experience of the divine is mediated, insofar as it necessarily involves some *medium by which* the object of perception is communicated or presented to the perceiver. Moreover, given that we are embodied beings, we might think that this medium will always involve some physical component, whether it be the activity of the brain, the physical and kinesthetic senses, or the body taken as an organic whole. There is, after all, *something that it is like to be an embodied creature experiencing the divine*, and this feature of theophanic experience is likely to be qualitatively different than it would be were we not embodied. Yet when theorists like Alston or Swinburne speak of "direct" and "immediate" experience, they do not appear to mean that it involves no bodily components or "feels." Rather, by "directness" they seem to mean that God is not perceived through the perception of any other object external to the person, and by "immediacy" that the beliefs arising out of this perception proceed noninferentially or in direct psychological proximity to the experience itself. Understood thusly, such experiences may still be mediated by bodily or other complex causal processes (Evans and Manis 2009: 105ff.).

However, there is a more interesting sense in which religious experience may be understood as materially mediated in a noetic sense. Here, I refer to the sensory, aesthetic, emotional, and/or kinesthetic experiences of external physical objects, artifacts, sounds, spaces, etc., *by means of which* a subject takes themself to experience divine or "ultimate" reality (or something about it) – for example, hearing God's voice in the recitation of a holy text or hearing sacred music, seeing God's creative power through observation of a natural landscape, feeling a sense of wonder while standing in a sacred space, cultivating a feeling of "creaturely dependence" through the repetition of ritualistic bodily movements, and so on. The tactile, olfactory, and gustatory senses can also play a significant role here. For example, touching, stroking, or kissing objects of devotion, smelling religious incense or other scents associated with worship, consuming the Eucharist or certain kinds of holy foods – these activities may all serve as a medium for the subjective apprehension of what is taken to be divine, otherworldly, or sacred.

These kinds of materially mediated experiences may be epistemologically relevant for defending the rationality of religious belief – or even for the enterprise of natural theology – especially when they are understood as *signs* concerning the existence or properties of the divine (Griffioen 2017). For example, to draw an analogy with the moral situation, it seems wholly possible that the embodied experience of certain objects or states of affairs, which need not themselves be specifically religious in nature, could assist the experiencing subject in picking out religiously salient facts in a particular situation – or even that theological facts may supervene on natural facts. Alternatively, a more semiotic approach might emphasize how material objects and artifacts can "point beyond themselves" to certain facts about God. As Evans notes, such experiences could provide either inferential or noninferential grounds for religious belief. For example, the observation of particular features of nature – e.g., a majestic landscape, the intricacies of cellular structure, the vastness of the night sky, etc. – may lead some to *infer* that God exists and intelligently designed the feature(s) in question. But for other, more "spiritually seasoned observers of the world," the divine reality might even present itself as an aspect, either hidden or plain, of the experience itself, where such observers are able to simply *see* the world *as* "God's handiwork" or to "read" God's existence directly off of nature (Evans 2011: 44).

A similar point has been made by Seyyed Hossein Nasr concerning the central notion of *āyāt* in the Qurʾan and its application in Sufism. He writes that, for the Sufi, "the universe is constituted of theophanies; the cosmos is a set of symbols to be contemplated and a means to reach the Symbolized, a book to be read and understood in both its outward and inward meanings"

(Nasr 2007: 46–47). Here, too, materially mediated religious experience may represent a starting point for discursive, evidential arguments for the existence of God, or it can serve as an occasion for the formation of immediate (perhaps "basic") religious beliefs via a kind of experiential "seeing as." In neither case is much won by insisting that religious experience be nonsensory, unless there is some other reason to think that nonsensory experience has a better or even exclusive claim to experiential religious knowledge.

Relatedly, in his discussion of how experiencing sacred spaces and music can be a way of cognizing the meaning of larger metaphysical and cosmological contexts, Mark Wynn has argued that philosophy of religion would do well to develop a corresponding epistemology that better acknowledges the sense-making capacities and affective responses of embodied human beings in a material sense (2013: 333–334). One such epistemology, as Muhammad Legenhausen (2013) has suggested, might explore how religious experience contributes to forms of religious *understanding*, as opposed to mere propositional knowledge, and to the virtue of *wisdom*, as opposed to mere rationality. As Legenhausen points out, knowledge is not the only epistemically valuable end at which epistemic agents aim, and rationality is not the only epistemic virtue in the game. In this sense, a religious epistemology that more thoroughly examines the role that understanding plays in the religious life and how religious wisdom contributes to or constitutes that understanding can perhaps provide an important supplement to standard knowledge-centered epistemologies and may even be able to better get at what makes the religious life epistemically valuable.

Importantly, understanding goes beyond merely justifiably believing some fact or set of facts and "getting things right" in so doing. Rather, it involves the ability to "see" or "grasp" how various related propositions hang together, what they mean, how they can be applied in various contexts, what their strengths and weaknesses are, and so on. As Catherine Elgin puts it, understanding is a matter of being able to "wield one's commitments to further one's epistemic ends" – to "draw inferences, raise questions, frame potentially fruitful inquiries, and so forth" (Elgin 2017: 3). In this sense, understanding is more *holistic*, and thereby more demanding, than the mere attainment or maintenance of piecemeal factual knowledge. In another sense, however, it may also be less demanding than propositional knowledge, at least if understanding need not be *factive* to represent an epistemic achievement, as I suggest in §5.21 below.

There are many forms of instrumental understanding relevant to the religious context. Within a particular tradition, one comes to grasp and successfully employ various religious concepts (including, perhaps, a particular model of

God, the divine, or ultimate reality), to read and comprehend sacred texts and narratives, to handle and use various liturgical objects and instruments in worship, to direct one's body and attentive faculties in certain ways, to cultivate certain emotions, and so on. But more fundamentally, religious understanding seems to involve a larger epistemic aim that is essentially *hermeneutical*. Whereas knowledge simply aims to "get things right" (in the right way), religious understanding involves an essentially interpretive venture aimed at *existential meaning and meaning-making*. Religions provide narrative cosmic frameworks from within which human beings come to better structure and grasp the meaning of their own experience *qua* human beings in the universe, as well as their relations to each other and the world around them – and to do so in ways that (ideally) contribute to the flourishing of all concerned. They allow us to "read meaning" off of our existence, so to speak, and to *orient* ourselves in ways that can make sense of the most fundamental aspects of that existence (Griffioen 2021).

It is obvious that religious experience – especially that of a materially mediated nature – plays a central role in the pursuit of such hermeneutical understanding, and one task of a future epistemology of religious experience will be to spell out how various kinds of experience contribute to the cultivation of forms of understanding that reflect and promote religious wisdom as it relates to this kind of existential meaning-making. An understanding-centered approach also makes room for a further exploration of the ways that the moral, social, historical, and political aspects of religion are fundamentally intertwined with its epistemic dimensions, which can allow for an opening up of religious epistemology to experiences, voices, and traditions it has tended to ignore. In this spirit, then, let us conclude this Element by briefly looking at a few of the ways in which the exploration of religious experience itself can be fruitfully expanded.

5.2 Rethinking Religious Experience

There are a number of ways in which philosophical explorations of religious experience can be productively expanded within an understanding-centered epistemology. Still, these considerations are not irrelevant for questions concerning the justification of religious belief, and philosophers who remain interested in defending the epistemic permissibility of believing religiously in today's world would also do well to think about forms of religious experience that go beyond the narrow focus on the nonsensory, passive, individual, episodic, remarkable, positively valenced, perceptual-like experiences that have dominated the literature.

5.2.1 From Belief to Acceptance: Nondoxastic Religious Experience

One upshot of a shift from theistic knowledge to religious understanding is that the latter arguably need not be factive in order to count as a cognitive achievement. Just as the sciences regularly employ models, idealizations, and what Elgin (2017) calls "felicitous falsehoods" that are not, strictly speaking, *true* in the pursuit of scientific understanding, there may be similarly epistemically relevant objects involved in religious understanding that do not match up one-to-one with reality. If this is right, then the heavily doxastic emphasis of philosophy of religion on religious *belief*, including experiential belief, may also need to be decentered. In some cases, all that may be needed for religious understanding is a sense of committed *acceptance* of particular propositions and concepts, not full-blown belief. (For discussions of nondoxastic acceptance, see not only Alston [1996] but also proponents of theological fictionalism and religious naturalism such as Wettstein [2012]; Jay [2014]; Deng [2015]; and Le Poidivin [2019].)

This is important because actual, committed religious practitioners come in all doxastic shapes and credences – from full conviction to an occasional lack of confidence to (sometimes profound) doubt to agnostic suspension and perhaps even disbelief. What cognitively unites such doxastically diverse participants is not necessarily their sharing the same *beliefs* but rather the ways in which they committedly employ shared religious *imaginings, models, and narratives* in their pursuit of a religious life of human flourishing. Indeed, even for "true believers," certain presuppositions that normally hold of reality may need to be imaginatively bracketed in order to take certain religious concepts and activities seriously (Luhrmann 2012), and this is likely to involve the use of the imagination in ways not dissimilar to how it functions in fictional or role-playing contexts, even if this "play" is of the most serious kind (Wagner 2014). With respect to religious experience, then, this opens the door for explorations of the possibility of *nondoxastic* religious experience – that is, religious experience that neither proceeds from nor immediately elicits religious belief. In fact, so long as it is possible to respond with genuine emotions to objects or situations we take to be fictional or nonliteral, it may likewise not seem implausible to attribute religious experiences of an emotional or affective kind to those who do not enjoy full-blown belief in the targets of such "fictional" emotions (Griffioen 2016). And it also seems plausible that these kinds of emotional religious experiences could still contribute to epistemically and theologically valuable understanding in the form of existential meaning-making, even if they do not always yield religious knowledge; it may even prime those who do not enjoy full credence for rational religious belief. If this is right, then, at the very least, the possibility of nondoxastic religious experience warrants increased philosophical attention.

5.2.2 From the Passive to the Active: Practice, Ritual, and Religious Experience

The emphasis on the doxastic aspects of religion has also resulted in the reinforcement of the Jamesian suggestion that religious experience is a largely *passive* matter, which has served to further isolate religious experiences and the epistemic insights won thereby from the actively pursued spiritual, devotional, and ritual practices which create the conditions for their occurrence. Yet if, with Stephen Bush, we think of religion itself more as a *social practice* and less as a collection of beliefs or doctrines, we not only avoid over-privileging credal religions such as Christianity, we are also better able to connect up experience, meaning, and power and to productively connect them to forms of widespread, collective human activity (2014: 191–194). Moreover, exploring the ways in which devotional practice and religious ritual not only serve to elicit various forms of religious experience but are also themselves relevantly experiential can help us resist construing religious experience as a wholly passive matter – and to do so in a way that both preserves and productively goes beyond the constructivist intuition that concepts precede and/or partially constitute our experience. Additionally, by showing how religious experience fundamentally depends on *human activity and agency*, we can explore how the experience of the religious "everyday" of repeated and habitual spiritual practice can be as epistemically and religiously significant for individuals as those extraordinary or remarkable experiences of religious "geniuses" upon which philosophers have tended to focus.

This can also help correct certain biases in Western philosophy of religion. For instance, there is a tendency to construe mysticism as revolving almost exclusively around individual mystical experiences of the quasi-Jamesian sort. Yet this fails to take into account the centrality in mystical texts of the relationship of such experience to both prior spiritual practice and the pursuit of the Good Life in communion with others (Griffioen and Zahedi 2018). Additionally, the way non-Christian traditions have been treated in the literature has also been skewed by an overemphasis on the cognitive. For example, much of the Western literature on Buddhist enlightenment experience neglects the fundamental roles that the ritual, textual, institutional, and sociopolitical play in the experiential aspect of Buddhism (Sharf 1995; Burton 2020). Likewise, philosophy of religion has largely ignored or outright dismissed traditions that make active use of entheogens such as peyote, psilocybin, animal venom, and the like in order to induce certain kinds of religious experience (cf. Wulff 1997: 91; Smith 2000; Cole-Turner 2015).

Finally, a focus on religious practice and ritual can also help philosophy of religion expand its horizons to include commonly neglected yet religiously significant emotions and experiential states beyond the feelings of wonder, amazement, joy, awe, or rapture typically associated with passive Jamesian-style experiences. To take just one example, Anastasia Philippa Scrutton has explored the significance of religious ritual in experiencing and cognizing *grief* among the Shona people in Zimbabwe and Paganist groups in the UK. Religious ritual, she argues, can help grieving individuals experience certain ideas surrounding loss and the afterlife *as real* via a kind of experiential cognition that Scrutton claims "goes beyond the propositional cognition offered by [mere] truth claims" (2017: 215). Similar investigation into the role of religious practice in cultivating other kinds of religiously relevant feelings and states is warranted, especially where they are common amongst practitioners on the ground and relevant for existential meaning-making and orientation.

5.2.3 From the Spiritual Senses to the Bodily Senses: The Somatics of Religious Experience

We have seen above how moving from nonsensory to sensory perceptual experience can be useful for both knowledge- and understanding-centered religious epistemologies. This will also mean increasing philosophical attention to the role of the body in such experience (Wynn 2018). Indeed, taking seriously the relationship of the perceptual to the somatic in religious experience allows for the integration of research from such fields as neuroscience, cognitive science, evolutionary biology, aesthetics, and kinesiology, among others, and to look at how topics such as embodied cognition, states of "flow," bodily motion, and the like are relevant for discussions of religious experience (Norris 2011; Tan 2016). It thus opens up room for positive engagement between philosophy of religion and other empirical and scientific disciplines that goes beyond merely addressing "debunking" arguments.

Perhaps even more importantly, the dismissal of bodily experience in philosophy of religion has also served to marginalize the experiences of certain individuals and groups, often along gender, racial, and sociocultural lines. For example, Western Christianity has tended historically to view women as more closely tied to their affective and corporeal natures – as more susceptible to sensation, passion, and emotion – and as more likely than men to be "intellectually compromised" by their bodies, leading to a general suspicion of their sensory and somatic religious experiences. Unfortunately, as Christina Van

Dyke has rightly noted, "the close negative association of bodies and emotions in women continues through to the present day" (2018: 160), and she plausibly argues that this negative association has contributed significantly to the ways mystical experience (and, we might add, theistic religious experience in general) has been defined and treated in the contemporary philosophical literature.

This philosophical dismissal of women's bodily experience is even more severe when it comes to black female bodies. Whereas white, predominantly European women are still cited in the philosophical literature (even if taken out of context and largely divorced from their bodies), the spiritual autobiographies of African-American women, a genre that often places embodied religious experience at the center of narratives concerning individual and community transformation, go almost completely ignored by philosophy of religion. On this point, Joy Bostic rightly notes that the delegitimization of African-American women's embodied knowledge and action in the scholarship on Western mysticism exhibits a disciplinary antagonism that informs "activities of direct and symbolic violence meted out against female, poor, and darker-skinned persons" (2013: 28).

For all these reasons, philosophy of religion would do well to both take pains to correct its bias against bodily experience in general and to begin to center voices and traditions that have been overlooked or discounted on the basis of their being historically negatively associated with corporeality.

5.2.4 From the Theistic to the Non(mono)theistic: Experiencing Things Other Than God

When we begin to include both religious practice and more embodied forms of religious experience in our analyses, we also start to make room for religious experiences beyond those taken to be perceptions of *God*. Indeed, the overemphasis in the analytic epistemological literature on experiences of the God of classical perfect-being theism serves to exclude a large swath of episodic experiences that appear to fall equally well under the rubric of religious experience.

First, practitioners of religious traditions sometimes characterized as "nontheistic," or in which the existence of gods plays a significantly less central role, quite obviously have religious experiences. Moreover, while many such experiences have been subsumed under what Stace (1960) called the *introvertive mystical experience* of "Oneness," or what Yandell (1993) classified as *nirvanic* and *kevalic* experiences, this certainly does not exhaust the vast kinds of experiences practitioners of such traditions may have, and it perhaps does them a disservice to assume this is the only kind of religious experience of any significance in these traditions. For example, as David Burton notes, visionary experiences of Buddhas and Bodhisattvas occupy a prominent position in Mahāyāna and Vajrayāna Buddhism and were often used by Mahāyāna Buddhists as evidence that their *sūtras* were not only authentic revelations of the Buddha but were "superior to those transmitted to other non-Mahāyāna traditions by the historical Buddha" (2020: 201). However, such experiences have seldom interested religious epistemologists.

Second, even in theistic traditions, there are experiences of phenomena and beings which are not themselves gods, or which may not provide information about any deity (though they may also do so), which go relatively overlooked. Nevertheless, such experiences seem relevant for philosophical analyses of religious experience, especially when concerned with the ways in which these experiences contribute centrally to religious understanding and meaning-making. Not only do such purported phenomena as prophetic dreams, near-death experiences, or the witnessing of the miraculous appear to constitute strong candidates for the philosophical treatment of religious experience (Bowie 2020), reports of the experiences of angels, demons, jinn, dead saints and prophets, ghosts, ancestors, and the like abound in various cultures, sometimes even among those who do not otherwise profess religious belief. For example, a study by Xinzhong Yao found that, despite the fact that the majority of Han Chinese in mainland China describe themselves as nonreligious or atheist, a whopping 21.2 percent of respondents claimed to have actually *experienced* the presence of their ancestors. The persistence of such experiences, despite their "having been criticized by generation after generation of revolutionaries throughout the 20th century" (Yao 2006: 53), points to the complicated relationships between religious profession, belief, and experience and should receive more attention from epistemologists of religion than they currently do. Placing these kinds of experience outside the purview of philosophical analysis by implicitly or explicitly painting them as mere instances of irrational "superstition" or "magical thinking" fails to take seriously their epistemic role in meaning-making and smacks of an overly rationalist – and, in some cases, implicitly colonialist – approach to religion, one which has been rightly criticized in religious studies and other fields but which remains dominant in many Anglo-American and European strands of philosophy of religion.

Third, treatments of the religious experiences of polytheistic religious movements or traditions that embrace or incorporate other kinds of deities than those of perfect-being monotheism are also sorely lacking in the epistemological literature. One notable counterexample is Jonathan Hill's (2020) recent exploration of the analytic theological implications of how British and American Wiccans experience certain pagan rituals, some involving what is taken to be literal spiritual possession. Likewise, scholars like Joy Bostic (2013), Jawanza

Eric Clark (2016), and Anthony B. Pinn (2017) have explored the way African-American religious experience (even of the Christian variety) has been influenced and shaped by nonmonotheistic Afro-Caribbean traditions. Still, little philosophical ink has been spilled on the epistemology of contemporary polytheistic or indigenous religious experience. The expansion of such studies could enrich the literature in religious epistemology both by giving philosophers a much larger data set of epistemically relevant experiences to draw from and by allowing for more detailed analyses of concrete manifestations of theistic experiences outside those of classical monotheism.

5.2.5 From the Positive to the Negative: Experiencing Evil and Absence

Of course, when we shift our attention from direct or indirect experiences of *God* on the classical monotheistic model of theism to experiences of other supernatural beings, otherworldly realms, and spiritual objects, we also open the door to religious experiences that are not necessarily positively valenced. To begin, allowing that the term "religious experience" can extend to experiences of *evil*, *wicked*, or *cursed* beings and spaces – e.g., of the demonic or Satanic, of incubi or succubae, of wicked tricksters or supernatural monsters, of malicious spirits, angry ghosts, or displeased ancestors, of hell, haunted spaces, or the dark side of the astral plane – means also allowing that religious experiences, even on the Jamesian model, may essentially involve negatively valenced emotions and attitudes. Fear, horror, dread, disgust, aversion, displeasure, anger, and the like represent common emotional reactions to the felt experience of wicked supernatural entities or accursed domains, and the epistemic role of such emotions is worth exploring in more philosophical depth. In this vein, William Abraham has recently argued that exorcisms and experiences of the devil "constitute striking evidence [. . .] for Christian theism" and "provide confirmation for a Christian vision of evil that is robust and accurate" (2021: 184) – claims that merit more discussion from both knowledge- and understanding-centered epistemologies.

   Of course, it need not always be *evil* beings that elicit a negatively valenced emotional experience. For example, the feeling of awe, a commonly cited religious emotion often associated with experience of the divine (cf., for example, Wettstein 2012; De Cruz 2020a), appears to represent a complex mixture of positive and negative affective components (Keltner and Haidt 2003; Arcangeli et al. 2020). Moreover, it is unclear that the spiritual, moral, and psychological *effects* of authentic religious experience always take the form of positive "fruits," as many philosophers have proposed. Someone who believes that they have been demonically possessed and who undergoes an exorcism may emerge from such an experience physically and emotionally scarred in ways that do not make them a better or more functional person. Alternatively, fear elicited by the experience of displeased ancestors or an angry deity may certainly motivate one to act in ways more consistent with the moral prescriptions of a particular religion, but it is unclear that action motivated solely by fear of punishment is really the kind of moral "fruit" philosophers tend to have in mind. It is also worth asking whether some experiences of God might even leave one morally or spiritually *worse off*. Is Job really "better off" in a spiritual sense for having had the kind of crushing religious experience he was forced to undergo by divine permission than had God simply left him alone in his previous life of virtue? He may end up repenting "in dust and ashes," but the text leaves open to interpretation whether the spiritual rift between him and God is ultimately repaired, as Nehama Verbin (2010, 2017) notes. She proposes that Job can be read as a Hasidic-inspired "knight of protest" who forgives but refuses to be reconciled with God and who "defeats what he takes to be divine abuse by protesting against it" (Verbin 2017: 383). Thus, the epistemology of religious experience may dovetail in interesting ways with questions of the problem of evil and theodicy.

Indeed, experiences of spiritual abuse or of horrendous evil in which God seems to be wholly absent are forms of experience that may lead to an irreparable fracturing of or schism in the human-divine relationship. Moreover, insofar as the various kinds of experiences of divine hiddenness may provide subjects with evidence – or even direct and immediate perceptions – of *divine absence*, they may likewise elicit not unreasonable negative beliefs about God or God's nature (e.g., that God does not exist or is not benevolent) and therefore may have some claim to be called religious experiences (Farennikova 2013). And their "fruits" – especially when they involve the kinds of spiritual trauma that result from abuse and the violation of trust by spiritual authorities – may, quite legitimately, be rejection, rebellion, or even deconversion (Panchuk 2018). Any philosophy of religious experience that wishes to explore the epistemic, spiritual, and moral effects of religious experience must therefore also be willing to look at the "dark side" of religious experience and to think carefully about how subjects' experiences of evil and divine hiddenness affect both what it is rational for such subjects to believe and how the meaning-making processes and understanding of the world thought to be fostered by religion may actually be undermined by such experiences.

5.2.6 From the Individual and Episodic to the Social and Dynamic: Collective and Collected Experience

Another sense in which analyses of religious experience can be expanded relies on the elasticity of the term "experience" itself. As we have seen, following

James, philosophers of religion have generally approached religious experience as something *individual* and *episodic*. That is, they look predominantly at singular, discrete events experienced by one particular subject at a particular time, with a relatively concrete beginning and end. Yet our use of the English term "experience" is much more flexible than this. First, it has applications in group as well as individual contexts. That is, experience seems to be something that can, in some contexts, be *collective* (Zahavi 2015). Second, it can refer to a kind of expertise or knowledge gained, or *collected*, over time as opposed to a discrete temporal event of limited duration. These various ways of talking about experience intersect in interesting ways.

First, episodic experience can be collective. Although we tend to index discrete experiences to individuals, it is also not unheard of to refer to group experience with respect to a particular episode – for example, the way the audience collectively experienced Stravinsky's *Rite of Spring* at its premiere or the collectively experienced joy the crowd expresses in response to a home run at a baseball game. While each individual present has their own experience of these events to which they can refer, when we speak about group experiences of these kinds we seem to mean something more than the mere conjunction of these individual experiences.

Second, individual experience may be diachronic. We often use the word "experienced" to describe individuals who have expertise, skill, or know-how acquired over time in a particular field or domain. So, for example, one may look for an "experienced midwife" when expecting one's first child or for an "experienced mechanic" when one's car needs repair. Moreover, the diachronic sense may additionally be used to refer to a certain kind of knowledge collected through various individual experiences over time (e.g., someone's experience during puberty, or with public transportation in Hong Kong, or as a jazz musician in Paris in the 1960s, etc.).

Finally, it is not uncommon to talk about the collective *and* collected experience of members of particular groups in particular contexts (e.g., the experience of Anishinaabe peoples in the nineteenth century, or women's experience in academia, or the experience of refugees in Germany since 2015). This use of "experience" not only refers to the common experiences of a group over time but also implies that there is *something that it is like* to be a member of the group in question and that members of that group are perhaps, given their collective and collected experience, *specially positioned* to speak authoritatively on that experience and the kinds of insight that arise from it.

Each of these senses of "experience" is relevant for philosophical discussions surrounding religious experience. We have already seen the ways in which rituals and religious practice are important for the cultivation of particular religious experiences of the episodic kind. Yet such practices rarely occur in isolation but are rather learned from, performed with, and even experientially shared by other members of the religious or spiritual community. They are social and communal, and, importantly, are not solely about the interior experience of the particular individual but also about the ways in which that experience is shared among or between members of a corporate religious body. Furthermore, such practices themselves, whether communal or performed in isolation, often exhibit a fundamentally *narrative structure* – one that is diachronic and experiential in nature and serves to place experiential episodes elicited by the ritual into a larger religious context. In this vein, we might think that the shared narratives involved in corporate religious practice can assist in providing a stable ground and relatively consistent shape to the dynamic and collectively shared experiential structures that ultimately manifest themselves in what Terence Cuneo has called "ritual knowledge" – that is, to the fundamental kind of *religious understanding* or *spiritual wisdom* that involves "knowing how to live in communion or be in rapport with" the divine or sacred, as well as with one's fellow human beings (2016: 166).

5.2.7 From Disagreement to Dialogue: Resonance, Dissonance, and the Promotion of Epistemic Justice

A further reason it is imperative to expand the philosophical discourse surrounding religious experience to collective and collected experience is that it can allow philosophy of religion and philosophical theology to better incorporate the voices of minority or marginalized groups and identities. First, it can provide us with a more open and ecumenical approach to the various ways that different religious groups construct meaning via the cultivation of particular kinds of religious experience. This can help bridge communicative gaps between majority and minority voices in the religious sphere, which may be crucial for the functioning of a plural society or for the coordination of joint political action. An understanding-centered epistemology that examines these possibilities can focus less on the supposed epistemic "duties" of individuals to adjust their credences in the face of disagreement and more on the *epistemic opportunities* presented by cultivating experiences of *resonance* between members of different religious traditions (Legenhausen 2013). Importantly, however, resonance does not entail consensus or agreement in belief on some matter. Rather, it is a particular kind of *reactive experience* by which acceptance is aroused and welcomed. It functions to allow one to better understand the space of another's reason in light of one's own. A more detailed philosophical analysis of resonance, therefore, has the potential to shift the discussion of religious difference from mere interreligious disagreement to include strategies for productive interfaith dialogue.

Second, this kind of philosophical expansion can help correct for a disciplinary form of what José Medina has called *epistemic arrogance*, which can arise within dominant groups whose cognitive authority represents the status quo within an epistemic domain. Such groups have little need to think about other perspectives and experiences and therefore "have but rare opportunities to find out their own limitations" (Medina 2013: 31–32). In philosophical contexts, the group whose voice is the loudest or whose presence is most heavily represented may come to assume that the perspective they positionally occupy is the only possible or relevant one, which can lead to a close-mindedness to alternative approaches and their dismissal as, for example, insufficiently "philosophical" or "rigorous." This dominant perspective of "assumed objectivity" (Haslanger 1993) can be epistemically limiting and harmful to both those in subordinated social positions and those who occupy positions of power. Subordinated persons are harmed by not being taken seriously as rational knowers, potentially leading to a silencing of their testimony and to increased difficulty in understanding their own experience (what Miranda Fricker [2007] has called *testimonial injustice* and *hermeneutic injustice*, respectively). Members of the dominant group, for their part, are harmed by their inability to perceive epistemically salient possibilities and alternatives, thereby closing themselves off to relevant perspectives and testimony that could potentially transmit knowledge. In the realm of religious experience, this can mean that the experience of particular groups or persons comes to be overlooked, discounted, or dismissed, on the grounds that it does not conform to the dominant philosophical model of religious experience or permit of "rational assessment" by that model's standards. For this reason, philosophers of religion may need to explicitly seek out discussions of religious experience from those traditionally neglected by the discipline, to introduce "epistemic frictions" into comfortable ways of thinking, and to be prepared to *center*, rather than tokenize, such discussions, in order to shift the equilibrium in the discipline to one that renders it more inclusive and welcoming of various forms of religious experience (Scheman 2011; De Cruz 2020b).

5.3 Concluding Thoughts: Experiencing the Discipline Differently

Certainly we don't want to expand the meaning of "religious experience" to signify anything and everything within the religious domain. However, if conceptual precision is maintained at the cost of excluding large swaths of the experiential dimension of the religious life, it is not clear that this is the kind of "rigor" the discipline ought to promote. Expanding the notion of religious experience in the above ways is not a matter of creating unnecessary conceptual "bloat." The better metaphor is that of *pregnancy*: The term "religious experience," like religion itself, is pregnant with meaning, and it is up to us to analyze its various facets and dimensions, to allow its meanings to gestate and grow as we explore them, and to develop innovative ways of approaching old debates that move the philosophy of religious experience forward in more fruitful and fecund ways. This may involve trying to develop a theoretical framework that better accommodates religious experience in all its messy plurality – and thinking more closely about how this complicated experiential dimension is intertwined with questions concerning religious meaning and social power. Or it may mean focusing on particular manifestations or types of religious experience in a particular context, either singly or from a comparative approach. Either way, we will need to be clear about *whose experiences* we are talking about, in *which context* they are situated, and to *what end* we are exploring them.

Indeed, a religious epistemology that goes beyond defending the mere rational permissibility of experiential theistic belief – one which concerns itself with the larger role of religious experience in the cultivation of religious understanding and wisdom – can be more ambitious than that discussed in previous sections. Not only can it put religious experience to use in further bolstering the plausibility of religious claims, as it has traditionally done; it can also demonstrate the significance of the experiential dimension of religion to human processes of existential meaning-making and use the insights won by such analyses to foster increased understanding about and between religious traditions. It can help shift the focus in philosophy of religion from disagreement to dialogue, from rationality indexed to generic individuals to the wisdom cultivated by particular communities, from difference-in-experience as an epistemic challenge to diversity-in-experience as an epistemic opportunity. Such an approach will not be easy, insofar as it attempts to do justice to the moral, social, political, material, embodied, and historical dimensions of religious experience, and it will require both the introduction of dissonances and the location of resonances. But it can also help the epistemology of religious experience move forward in ways that genuinely display the love of wisdom that *philo-sophia* seeks to embody.

References

Abraham, William J. 2012. "Analytic Philosophers of Religion." In Paul L. Gavrilyuk & Sarah Coakley (eds.), *The Spiritual Senses: Perceiving God in Western Christianity*, 275–290. Cambridge: Cambridge University Press.

2021. "Divine Action and the Demonic." In *Divine Agency and Divine Action, Volume IV*, 168–184. Oxford: Oxford University Press.

Alston, William P. 1993. *Perceiving God: The Epistemology of Religious Experience*. Ithaca, NY: Cornell University Press.

1996. "Belief, Acceptance, and Religious Faith." In Jeff Jordan & Daniel Howard-Snyder (eds.), *Faith, Freedom and Rationality: Essays in the Philosophy of Religion*, 3–27. Lanham, MD: Rowman & Littlefield.

Arcangeli, Margherita, Marco Sperduti, Amélie Jacquot, Pascale Piolino, & Jérôme Dokic. 2020. "Awe and the Experience of the Sublime: A Complex Relationship." *Frontiers in Psychology* 11, 1340–1345.

Asad, Talal. 1993. *Genealogies of Religion: Discipline and Reasons of Power in Christianity and Islam*. Baltimore, MD: Johns Hopkins University Press.

Barrett, Justin L. 2007. "Is the Spell Really Broken? Bio-Psychological Explanations of Religion and Theistic Belief." *Theology and Science* 5(1), 57–72.

2011. *Cognitive Science, Religion, and Theology: From Human Minds to Divine Minds*. West Conshohocken, PA: Templeton Press.

Bostic, Joy R. 2013. *African American Female Mysticism: Nineteenth-Century Religious Activism*. New York: Palgrave Macmillan.

Bowie, Fiona. 2020. "Miraculous and Extraordinary Events as Religious Experience." In Paul K. Moser & Chad V. Meister (eds.), *The Cambridge Companion to Religious Experience*, 261–283. Cambridge: Cambridge University Press.

Brown, David. 2004. *God and Enchantment of Place: Reclaiming Human Experience*. Oxford: Oxford University Press.

Buckareff, Andrei A. & Yujin Nagasawa (eds.). 2016. *Alternative Concepts of God: Essays on the Metaphysics of the Divine*. Oxford: Oxford University Press.

Burton, David. 2020. "Religious Experience in Buddhism." In Paul K. Moser & Chad V. Meister (eds.), *The Cambridge Companion to Religious Experience*, 187–207. Cambridge: Cambridge University Press.

Bush, Stephen S. 2014. *Visions of Religion: Experience, Meaning, and Power.* New York: Oxford University Press.

Clark, Jawanza Eric. 2016. *Indigenous Black Theology: Toward an African-Centered Theology of the African-American Religious Experience.* New York: Palgrave Macmillan.

Coakley, Sarah. 2009. "Dark Contemplation and Epistemic Transformation: The Analytic Theologian Re-Meets Teresa of Avila." In Oliver Crisp & Michael Rea (eds.), *Analytic Theology: New Essays in the Philosophy of Theology*, 280–312. Oxford: Oxford University Press.

Cole-Turner, Ron. 2015. "Spiritual Enhancement." In Calvin R. Mercer & Tracy J. Trothen (eds.), *Religion and Transhumanism: The Unknown Future of Human Enhancement*, 369–384. Santa Barbara, CA: Praeger Publishers.

Cottingham, John. 2005. *The Spiritual Dimension: Religion, Philosophy, and Human Value.* Cambridge: Cambridge University Press.

Cuneo, Terence. 2016. *Ritualized Faith: Essays on the Philosophy of Liturgy.* Oxford: Oxford University Press.

De Cruz, Helen. 2020a. "Awe and Wonder in Scientific Practice: Implications for the Relationship between Science and Religion." In Michael Fuller, Dirk Evers, Anne Runehov, Knut-Willy Sæther, & Bernard Michollet (eds.), *Issues in Science and Theology: Nature – and Beyond*, 155–168. Cham: Springer International.

2020b. "Seeking out Epistemic Friction in the Philosophy of Religion." In Michelle Panchuk & Michael Rea (eds.), *Voices from the Edge: Centring Marginalized Perspectives in Analytic Theology*, 23–46. Oxford: Oxford University Press.

Deng, Natalja. 2015. "Religion for Naturalists." *International Journal for Philosophy of Religion* 78(2), 195–214.

Dole, Andrew. 2004. "Schleiermacher and Otto on Religion." *Religious Studies* 40(4), 389–413.

2016. "What is 'Religious Experience' in Schleiermacher's Dogmatics, and Why Does It Matter?" *Journal of Analytic Theology* 4(1), 44–65.

Dols, Michael W. 1992. *Majnun: The Madman in Medieval Islamic Society.* Oxford: Clarendon Press.

Elgin, Catherine Z. 2017. *True Enough.* Cambridge, MA: MIT Press.

Eliade, Mircea. 1958. *Patterns in Comparative Religion.* New York: Sheed and Ward.

1987. *The Sacred and the Profane: The Nature of Religion.* Orlando, FL: Harcourt Brace.

Evans, C. Stephen. 2010. *Natural Signs and Knowledge of God: A New Look at Theistic Arguments.* Oxford: Oxford University Press.

2011. "Religious Experience and the Question of Whether Belief in God Requires Evidence." In Kelly James Clark & Raymond J. VanArragon (eds.), *Evidence and Religious Belief*, 37–51. Oxford: Oxford University Press.

Evans, C. Stephen & R. Zachary Manis. 2009. *Philosophy of Religion: Thinking about Faith*. Downers Grove, IL: InterVarsity Press.

Fales, Evan. 1996a. "Mystical Experience as Evidence." *International Journal for Philosophy of Religion* 40(1), 19–46.

1996b. "Scientific Explanations of Mystical Experiences, I: The Case of St Teresa." *Religious Studies* 32(2), 143–163.

1996c. "Scientific Explanations of Mystical Experiences, II: The Challenge of Theism." *Religious Studies* 32(3), 297–313.

1999. "Can Science Explain Mysticism?" *Religious Studies* 35(2), 213–227.

Farennikova, Anna. 2013. "Seeing Absence." *Philosophical Studies* 166(3), 429–454.

Forman, Robert K. C. 1986. "Pure Consciousness Events and Mysticism." *Sophia* 25(1), 49–58.

1999. *Mysticism, Mind, Consciousness*. Albany: State University of New York Press.

Franks Davis, Caroline. 1989. *The Evidential Force of Religious Experience*. Oxford: Oxford University Press.

Fricker, Miranda. 2007. *Epistemic Injustice: Power and the Ethics of Knowing*. Oxford: Oxford University Press.

Gale, Richard M. 1991. *On the Nature and Existence of God*. Cambridge: Cambridge University Press.

Gellman, Jerome. 1998. "On a Sociological Challenge to the Veridicality of Religious Experience." *Religious Studies* 34(3), 235–251.

2001. *Mystical Experience of God: A Philosophical Inquiry*. New York: Routledge.

2010. "A Problem for the Christian Mystical Doxastic Practice." *Philo* 13(1), 23–28.

Griffioen, Amber L. 2016. "Religious Experience without Belief? Toward an Imaginative Account of Religious Engagement." In Thomas Hardtke, Ulrich Schmiedel, & Tobias Tan (eds.), *Religious Experience Revisited: Expressing the Inexpressible?*, 73–88. Leiden: Brill.

2017. "'Signs for a People Who Reason': Religious Experience and Natural Theology." *European Journal for Philosophy of Religion* 9(2), 139–163.

2021 [forthcoming]. "Rethinking Religious Epistemology." *European Journal for Philosophy of Religion*.

Griffioen, Amber L. & Mohammad Sadegh Zahedi. 2018. "Medieval Christian and Islamic Mysticism and the Problem of a 'Mystical Ethics.'" In Thomas Williams (ed.), *The Cambridge Companion to Medieval Ethics*, 280–305. Cambridge: Cambridge University Press.

Guthrie, Stewart. 1993. *Faces in the Clouds: A New Theory of Religion*. Oxford: Oxford University Press.

Harris, Harriet A. 2005. "Does Analytical Philosophy Clip Our Wings? Reformed Epistemology as a Test Case." In Harriet A. Harris & Christopher J. Insole (eds.), *Faith and Philosophical Analysis: The Impact of Analytical Philosophy on the Philosophy of Religion*, 100–118. Burlington, VT: Ashgate.

Haslanger, Sally. 1993. "On Being Objective and Being Objectified." In Louise M. Antony & Charlotte Witt (eds.), *A Mind of One's Own: Feminist Essays on Reason and Objectivity*, 209–253. Boulder, CO: Westview Press.

Heriot-Maitland, Charles P. 2008. "Mysticism and Madness: Different Aspects of the Same Human Experience?", *Mental Health, Religion & Culture* 11(3), 301–325.

Heschel, Abraham J. 1983. *God in Search of Man: A Philosophy of Judaism*. New York: Farrar, Straus, & Giroux.

Hick, John. 1989. *An Interpretation of Religion: Human Responses to the Transcendent*. Basingstoke: Palgrave Macmillan.

2006. *The New Frontier of Religion and Science: Religious Experience, Neuroscience and the Transcendent*. Basingstoke: Palgrave Macmillan.

Hill, Jonathan. 2020. "'I Am the Gracious Goddess': Wiccan Analytic Theology." *Journal of Analytic Theology* 8(1), 152–177.

Hood, Ralph W. 2001. *Dimensions of Mystical Experiences: Empirical Studies and Psychological Links*. Amsterdam: Rodopi.

James, William. 2002. *Varieties of Religious Experience: A Study in Human Nature*. London: Routledge.

Jantzen, Grace. 1984. *God's World, God's Body*. London: Darton Longman & Todd.

1994. "Feminists, Philosophers, and Mystics." *Hypatia* 9(4), 186–206.

1995. *Power, Gender and Christian Mysticism*. Cambridge: Cambridge University Press.

Jay, Christopher. 2014. "The Kantian Moral Hazard Argument for Religious Fictionalism." *International Journal for Philosophy of Religion* 75(3), 207–232.

Joas, Hans. 2011. "Schleiermacher and the Turn to Experience in the Study of Religion." In Dietrich Korsch & Amber L. Griffioen (eds.), *Interpreting*

Religion: The Significance of Friedrich Schleiermacher's "Reden über die Religion" for Religious Studies and Theology, 147–161. Tübingen: Mohr Siebeck.

Katz, Steven T. 1978. "Language, Epistemology, and Mysticism." In Steven T. Katz (ed.), *Mysticism and Philosophical Analysis*, 22–74. Oxford: Oxford University Press.

    1992. "Mystical Speech and Mystical Meaning." In Steven T. Katz (ed.), *Mysticism and Language*, 3–41. New York: Oxford University Press.

Kelemen, Deborah. 2004. "Are Children 'Intuitive Theists'? Reasoning about Purpose and Design in Nature." *Psychological Science* 15(5), 295–301.

Kelemen, Deborah & Evelyn Rosset. 2009. "The Human Function Compunction: Teleological Explanation in Adults." *Cognition* 111(1), 138–143.

Keltner, Dacher & Jonathan Haidt. 2003. "Approaching Awe, a Moral, Spiritual, and Aesthetic Emotion." *Cognition and Emotion* 17(2), 297–314.

Legenhausen, Muhammad. 2013. "Responding to the Religious Reasons of Others: Resonance and Nonreductive Religious Pluralism." *European Journal for Philosophy of Religion* 5(2), 23–46.

Le Poidevin, Robin. 2019. *Religious Fictionalism*. Cambridge: Cambridge University Press.

Lipsedge, Maurice. 1996. "Religion and Madness in History." In Dinesh Bhugra (ed.), *Psychiatry and Religion: Context, Consensus and Controversies*, 23–50. London: Routledge.

Luhrmann, Tanya M. 2012. *When God Talks Back: Understanding the American Evangelical Relationship with God*. New York: Vintage Books.

Mackie, John L. 1982. *The Miracle of Theism: Arguments For and Against the Existence of God*. Oxford: Clarendon Press.

Mariña, Jacqueline. 2008. "Friedrich Schleiermacher and Rudolf Otto." In John Corrigan (ed.), *The Oxford Handbook of Religion and Emotion*, 457–473. Oxford: Oxford University Press.

Mavrodes, George I. 1970. *Belief in God: A Study in the Epistemology of Religion*. Washington, DC: University Press of America.

Mawson, Tim J. 2006. "God's Body." *The Heythrop Journal* 47(2), 171–181.

McCutcheon, Russell T. 1997. *Manufacturing Religion: The Discourse on Sui Generis Religion and the Politics of Nostalgia*. Oxford: Oxford University Press.

    2012. *Critics Not Caretakers: Redescribing the Public Study of Religion*. Ithaca, NY: SUNY Press.

McFague, Sallie. 1993. *The Body of God: An Ecological Theology.* Minneapolis, MN: Fortress Press.

Medina, José. 2013. *The Epistemology of Resistance: Gender and Racial Oppression, Epistemic Injustice, and Resistant Imaginations.* Oxford: Oxford University Press.

Murray, Michael. 2008. "Four Arguments that the Cognitive Psychology of Religion Undermines the Justification of Religious Belief." In Joseph Abdul Bulbulia, Richard Sosis, Erica Harris, Russell Genet, Cheryl Genet, & Karen Wyman (eds.), *The Evolution of Religion: Studies, Theories & Critiques*, 365–370. Santa Margarita, CA: Collins Foundation Press.

Nasr, Seyyed Hossein. 2007. *The Garden of Truth: The Vision and Promise of Sufism, Islam's Mystical Tradition.* New York: HarperOne.

Nichols, Ryan. 2014. "Thomas Reid." In Graham Oppy & Nick Trakakis (eds.), *Early Modern Philosophy of Religion*, 235–248. Abingdon-on-Thames: Routledge.

Norris, Rebecca Sachs. 2011. "Religion, Neuroscience and Emotion: Some Implications of Consumerism and Entertainment Culture." In David Cave & Rebecca Sachs Norris (eds.), *Religion and the Body*, 105–128. Leiden: Brill.

Otto, Rudolf. 2004. *Das Heilige: Über das Irrationale in der Idee des Göttlichen und sein Verhältnis zum Rationalen.* Munich: Beck.

Panchuk, Michelle. 2018. "The Shattered Spiritual Self: A Philosophical Exploration of Religious Trauma." *Res Philosophica* 95(3), 505–530.

Pargament, Kenneth I. 2013a. "Searching for the Sacred: Toward a Nonreductionistic Theory of Spirituality." In Kenneth I. Pargament (ed.), *APA Handbook of Psychology, Religion, and Spirituality*, 257–273. Washington, DC: American Psychological Association.

2013b. "Spirituality as an Irreducible Human Motivation and Process." *International Journal for the Psychology of Religion* 23(4), 271–281.

Pinn, Anthony B. 2017. *Varieties of African American Religious Experience: Toward a Comparative Black Theology*, twentieth anniversary edition. Minneapolis, MN: Fortress Press.

Plantinga, Alvin. 2000. *Warranted Christian Belief.* New York: Oxford University Press.

Potter, Dennis (Kelli). 2013. "Religious Disagreement: Internal and External." *International Journal for Philosophy of Religion* 74(1), 21–31.

Potter, Kelli. [forthcoming]. "The Significance of Heterodoxy." In Brian Birch & Patrick Horn (eds.), *Radical Pluralism in Ethics and Religion*. Tübingen: Mohr Siebeck.

Proudfoot, Wayne. 1985. *Religious Experience*. Berkeley: University of California Press.

Quinn, Philip L. 1995. "Towards Thinner Theologies: Hick and Alston on Religious Diversity." *International Journal for Philosophy of Religion* 38, 145–164.

Raphael, Melissa. 1994. "Feminism, Constructivism and Numinous Experience." *Religious Studies* 30(4), 511–526.

Scheman, Naomi. 2011. "Queering the Center by Centering the Queer: Reflections on Transsexuals and Secular Jews." In Naomi Scheman (ed.), *Shifting Ground: Knowledge and Reality, Transgression and Trustworthiness*, 111–144. Oxford: Oxford University Press.

Schleiermacher, Friedrich. 1996. *On Religion: Speeches to Its Cultured Despisers*, translated and edited by Richard Crouter. Cambridge: Cambridge University Press.

    2016. *The Christian Faith*, translated by Paul T. Nimmo. London: Bloomsbury T&T Clark.

Schmidt, Leigh Eric. 2003. "The Making of Modern 'Mysticism.'". *Journal of the American Academy of Religion* 71(2), 273–302.

Scott, Joan Wallach. 1991. "The Evidence of Experience." *Critical Inquiry* 17 (4), 773–797.

Scrutton, Anastasia Philippa. 2017. "Grief, Ritual and Experiential Knowledge: A Philosophical Perspective." In Dennis Klass & Edith Maria Steffen (eds.), *Continuing Bonds in Bereavement: New Directions for Research and Practice*, 214–226. London: Routledge.

Shanon, Benny. 2002. *The Antipodes of the Mind: Charting the Phenomenology of the Ayahuasca Experience*. Oxford: Oxford University Press.

Sharf, Robert. 1995. "Buddhist Modernism and the Rhetoric of Meditative Experience." *Numen* 42(3), 228–283.

    1998. "Experience." In Mark C. Taylor (ed.), *Critical Terms for Religious Studies*, 94–116. Chicago, IL and London: University of Chicago Press.

Sluhovsky, Moshe. 2007. *Believe Not Every Spirit: Possession, Mysticism, and Discernment in Early Modern Catholicism*. Chicago, IL: University of Chicago Press.

Smart, Ninian. 1965. "Interpretation and Mystical Experience." *Religious Studies* 1(1), 75–87.

Smith, Huston. 2000. *Cleansing the Doors of Perception: The Religious Significance of Entheogenic Plants and Chemicals*. New York: Putnam Inc.

Stace, Walter T. 1960. *Mysticism and Philosophy*. Toronto: Palgrave Macmillan.

Swinburne, Richard. 2004. *The Existence of God*. Oxford: Clarendon Press.

Tan, Tobias. 2016. "The Corporeality of Religious Experience: Embodied Cognition in Religious Practices." In Thomas Hardtke, Ulrich Schmiedel, & Tobias Tan (eds.), *Religious Experience Revisited: Expressing the Inexpressible?*, 207–226. Leiden: Brill.

Taves, Ann. 2009. *Religious Experience Reconsidered: A Building Block Approach to the Study of Religion and Other Special Things*. Princeton: Princeton University Press.

Tillich, Paul. 1973. *Systematic Theology: Volume One*. Chicago, IL: University of Chicago Press.

Underhill, Evelyn. 1912. *Mysticism, A Study: The Nature and Development of Man's Spiritual Consciousness*. New York: E. P. Dutton and Co.

Van Dyke, Christina. 2018. "What Has History to Do with Philosophy? Insights From the Medieval Contemplative Tradition." *Proceedings of the British Academy* 214, 155–170.

  2022 [forthcoming]. "From Meditation to Contemplation: Broadening the Borders of Philosophy in the 13th–15th Centuries." In Amber L. Griffioen & Marius Backmann (eds.), *Pluralizing Philosophy's Past: New Reflections in the History of Philosophy*. Cham: Palgrave Macmillan/ Springer International.

van Eyghen, Hans. 2020. *Arguing from Cognitive Science of Religion: Is Religious Belief Debunked?* London: Bloomsbury Academic.

van Leeuwen, Neil & Michiel van Elk. 2019. "Seeking the Supernatural: The Interactive Religious Experience Model." *Religion, Brain & Behavior* 9 (3), 221–251.

Verbin, Nehama. 2010. *Divinely Abused: A Philosophical Perspective on Job and His Kin*. London: Continuum International Publishing.

  2017. "Three Knights of Faith on Job's Suffering and its Defeat." *International Journal of Philosophy and Theology* 78(4–5), 382–395.

Wagner, Rachel. 2014. "The Importance of Playing in Earnest." In Heidi A. Campbell & Gregory P. Grieve (eds.), *Playing with Religion in Digital Games*, 192–213. Bloomington: Indiana University Press.

Wainwright, William J. 1973. "Mysticism and Sense Perception." *Religious Studies* 9(3), 257–278.

Webb, Mark Owen. 2015. *A Comparative Doxastic-Practice Epistemology of Religious Experience*. Cham: Springer International.

Wettstein, Howard K. 2012. *The Significance of Religious Experience*. New York: Oxford University Press.

Wildman, Wesley J. 2011. *Religious and Spiritual Experiences*. Cambridge: Cambridge University Press.

Wulff, David M. 1997. *Psychology of Religion: Classic and Contemporary.* New York: John Wiley & Sons.

Wynn, Mark. 2012. "Re-Enchanting the World: The Possibility of Materially-Mediated Religious Experience." In Robert MacSwain (ed.), *Theology, Aesthetics, and Culture: Responses to the Work of David Brown*, 115–127. Oxford: Oxford University Press.

2013. "Religious Experience and Natural Theology." In Russell Re Manning (ed.), *The Oxford Handbook of Natural Theology*, 325–339. Oxford: Oxford University Press.

2018. "Aesthetic Goods and the Nature of Religious Understanding." In Fiona Ellis (ed.), *New Models of Religious Understanding*, 116–133. Oxford: Oxford University Press.

Yadav, Sameer. 2015. *The Problem of Perception and the Experience of God: Toward a Theological Empiricism.* Minneapolis, MN: Fortress Press.

2016. "Mystical Experience and the Apophatic Attitude." *Journal of Analytic Theology* 4(1), 17–43.

Yandell, Keith E. 1993. *The Epistemology of Religious Experience.* Cambridge: Cambridge University Press.

Yao, Xinzhong. 2006. "Religious Experience in Contemporary China." *Modern Believing* 47(2), 44–61.

Zahavi, D. 2015. "You, Me, and We: The Sharing of Emotional Experiences." *Journal of Consciousness Studies* 22(1–2), 84–101.

Acknowledgments

I am grateful to Lacey Hudspeth, Christina Van Dyke, Julia Boll, Jessica Engelking, Kim Halvorson, the "refuge" message group, and especially to the Academic Women's Online Writing Retreat for their support and encouragement in the writing of this Element during a time of pandemic, unemployment, loss, pregnancy, birth, and transition. Thanks also to Roderich Barth, Dan Boscaljon, Jochen Briesen, Dina Emundts, Dietrich Korsch, Jörg Lauster, and Mohammad Sadegh Zahedi for the many discussions on ideas related to this topic over the years, as well as to Yujin Nagasawa for his patience and to an anonymous reviewer for their helpful comments. This book is dedicated to Daniel and to our rainbow baby girl, Charlie Rae.

Cambridge Elements ≡

Philosophy of Religion

Yujin Nagasawa

University of Birmingham

Yujin Nagasawa is Professor of Philosophy and Co-Director of the John Hick Centre for Philosophy of Religion at the University of Birmingham. He is currently President of the British Society for the Philosophy of Religion. He is a member of the editorial board of *Religious Studies*, the *International Journal for Philosophy of Religion* and *Philosophy Compass*.

About the Series

This Cambridge Elements series provides concise and structured introductions to all the central topics in the philosophy of religion. It offers balanced, comprehensive coverage of multiple perspectives in the philosophy of religion. Contributors to the series are cutting-edge researchers who approach central issues in the philosophy of religion. Each provides a reliable resource for academic readers and develops new ideas and arguments from a unique viewpoint.

Cambridge Elements ≡

Philosophy of Religion

A full series listing is available at: www.cambridge.org/EPREL

Printed in the United States
by Baker & Taylor Publisher Services